Wonder*ache*

by
John Roedel

Wonderache by John Roedel

For permissions contact: john@johnroedel.com
Author Website: www.johnroedel.com

Cover photo by golden_designs1 www.fiverr.com/golden_designs1

ISBN: 9798338314494

To Linda Abrams who is the very definition of a wonder seeker.

Linda, thank you for showing us all how to live with wide open hearts and eyes. You are a burst of sunlight that warms all of our paths. What a blessing it is to be alive during your era. Your authentic soul must have been one of the first ones formed as the Universe cooled.

I am so grateful for your joy walking wisdom and grace you exhale. You have changed my life and the lives of so many. How lucky are we?

Welcome to Wonder*ache*

Hello, my fellow seeker! Welcome to my book of little wonderings. I'm so grateful you are here. Hold my hand as we walk into the wild woods together. The unknown is always less scary when we don't face it alone.

In my very first book, *"Hey God. Hey John."* I began to explore the idea that perhaps there was more for me to discover about the Divine than I had ever imagined. These conversations with "God" helped me safely navigate my unfolding faith crisis. That book was the first step on this new path of spiritual expansion I now find myself on. I penned hundreds of these dialogues before the format eventually transformed into poetry.

I am as shocked as anyone that these poems came from me.

This book of poetry isn't a map or a gospel. There are no answers or theology in these pages. There is only curiosity and the curviest of question marks for us to climb. I am not asking anyone to untether themselves from their spiritual beliefs or practiced faith. These poems aren't an attack on religion. They are simply an honest admission that my Catholic heart has melted into a formless pool of relentless curiosity.

I know I am not alone in this particular spiritual journey. Today, more than ever, many people find themselves wandering off the spiritual paths they once walked and into the fog of the unknown.

Thank you for joining me. This will be quite an adventure.

Let's explore our hearts together. Let's get lost in the backcountry of our souls. Let's follow the rivers inside of ourselves that lead to the ocean of unending mystery. Let's listen to the wind sing us holy songs through the pines as we sit by the crackling campfire.

Let's be brave. Let's be brave. Oh, my love, let's be so very brave as we ache for the wonder that surrounds us. Let's get started!

my fellow seeker,

you are invited to come wander into
the great mystery of this life with me.

please pack as many questions
as you can carry.

yes, I know that walking into the fog of
the unknown will be so scary -
but I also know that if we will both be
less afraid if we are holding hands

My love,

I feel like we are about to get so very lost
-   ~yet the more I think about it
if we stick together -
how lost can we actually get?

A Prelude to Wonder*ment*

When I was a child, I remember recoiling every time I was asked by a well-intentioned adult "what I wanted to be" when I grew up.

I used to answer honestly, "Nothing. I plan on being a kid my entire life."

"Oh, that's so cute," the adult would often reply. "Stay a child as long as you can!"

I humbly agreed with that sentiment. I had no interest in giving the cliched answers of "Fireman, Astronaut, or President of the USA." Even as a little child those vocations never held much interest to me.

I have always had a strange connection with Alice, who as you might remember, fell down a rabbit hole into a magical world she would explore and grow to love.

I wasn't at all curious about what I would "become" in the future. I was only invested in who I was in the present.. I didn't care about anything but chasing the bouncing rabbit of the moment into whatever new adventure was waiting for me around the corner. I considered myself a card-carrying resident misfit who would always be a proud resident of Wonderland.

As I grew into my teen years I usually couldn't make it a week without some adult posing the same question to me - however, during this time of my life, the probing was always wrapped in a bit more barbed wire than it had been before.

"What are you going to do after graduation?"
"What colleges are you applying to?"
"What are you going to major in?
"Have you given any more thought to what you want to do with the rest of your life?"

Unlike my peers at the time, I never could find any excitement in providing an answer to those sorts of inquiries. However, I discovered pretty quickly that saying "I want to remain a child" was not an acceptable answer to those questions. When I would respond with anything other than what was expected of me it would often lead to extra sessions with my guidance counselor and concerned looks from my parents.

Apparently, Wonderland has an age limit.

Eventually, I figured out that the more I lied and answered with "Accountant, Journalist, Lawyer, etc. - the fewer follow-up questions I would endure. I learned to just say whatever it was that people wanted to hear.

Now that I'm one of those dreaded adults myself I understand why I was being asked to answer those types of questions over and over. Those folks were just trying to help me come up with a map for the rest of my life. They were simply attempting to guide me to give my future some serious consideration.

Unfortunately for these dogs, they were barking up the wrong tree.

The truth was I never had any interest in "being" something. To write a script for the next 80 years of my existence on this spinning cosmic marble was an exercise that left me feeling nauseous every single time I attempted it.

I didn't want a plan to follow. I didn't want to "become" anything. I desired to simply be who I was in the present moment without worrying about who I might be tomorrow. After all, I thought, living like that seemed like it would allow for more surprises and adventure to come my way.

I refused to leave Neverland - and even now that I'm faced with turning 50-years-old, I am proud to say it remains my home still.

Now, of course, as you can imagine, this type of philosophy of not having any concrete life plans has caused me various moments of heartache over the years. Our world is built for people who know exactly where they are going and how they are going to get there. It's not an easy planet for a Lost Boy like myself who never became engrossed in choosing a life path - but, who instead, decided to keep everything an open-ended possibility.

While most of the kids I grew up with became doctors, sheriffs, engineers, CEOs, and lawyers - I have lived the past decades by "living in the moment" without anchoring myself to any single shoreline. Instead, I have chosen to remain untethered to a dock - and I have drifted in and out of dozens of vocations.

During my life, I have had the following jobs:

Youth Leader at a Church

Pharmacy Technician

Small Business Owner

Congressional Communication Officer

Improv Trainer

Travel Agent

Stand-Up Comedian

Crime Journalist

Poet (right now!)

It's all been a bit of vocational whiplash, that in hindsight, has absolutely increased the difficulty setting of my life. Had I just answered the question in my childhood and picked a life-path to follow, I wouldn't have faced so many long dark nights while wandering in Neverland.

This type of wanderlust has not just been confined to my vocational life. Over the past few years, this untethering has bled over into my spiritual life. I am a born and raised Catholic who has recently left that paved road of organized religion for the wilds of uncharted spiritual exploration.

I used to have standard answers/responses whenever I got into conversations about God. I would just rely on the script on spirituality I was given years ago during Sunday School and regurgitate those same answers to whomever I was talking to.

Turns out I was being a bit of a hypocrite.

While I was living my vocational life without any guardrails or compass to guide me - I found myself marching in line with all of my other fellow Catholic ants on our way to our promised eternal reward. Unlike my earthly existence, I was constantly worried about the future of my soul. So, I never questioned anything I had been told about the Divine and remained in the ant parade toward heaven.

That all changed a few years ago when I discovered the poetry that had been lying dormant in my heart for decades.

I never imagined I would have ever become a poet. It wasn't a literary genre I read or had ever had any particular interest in studying. Just one day, out of the blue, poems started pouring out of my little penguin fingers and out onto the computer screen. These words emerged from my heart like a wildflower on a bustling Manhattan sidewalk.

Becoming a poet has been such an unexpected journey for me. Yet, due to my Lost Boy ways, it wasn't something I questioned. I just said "Yes!" to poetry flowing out of me. I don't believe that would have happened had I cast my life in concrete. Being untied to any kind of hard and fast life plan gave me the freedom to embrace what was happening inside of me.

What I didn't expect was how these poems I was writing would start to untangle the knots to organized religion I was tied to. This poetry that was emerging from me challenged me to step out of any parade and go straight into the woods of spiritual mystery and wonderment.

Once I have opened my heart to other ways of experiencing spirituality, I formed a much closer relationship with the Unseen Mystery. I was no longer as concerned with the salvation of my soul as my daily pursuit of miracles and wonderment. I am no longer conversing with the Great Love while sitting with my hands folded in a church pew - I am connecting with the Divine in rainstorms, by serving others and through exploring previously uncharted areas of my heart through my poetry.

My whole life I have resisted the concept that I would need to "become" or "change" to fit the standards of our mad world. I wanted to stay free to be able to discover parts of my soul I didn't know existed. I didn't want to put myself in a box that I couldn't escape from.

Yet, I was content putting God in a box. *Like I said, I was being a hypocrite.*

These days, I am allowing my relationship with God to have the same freedom I have so desired for my vocational life. I am allowing my spirituality to surprise me every day. I am allowing for the Divine to reveal itself to me in whatever form it arrives in. I am allowing for doubt. I am allowing for mystery. I am allowing myself to find God in places I had never considered before.

Now, after 48-years, I feel like I am actually starting to "become" something. I am becoming a better witness to the Divine. I am becoming a seeker. I am becoming a joyful spiritual wanderer.

I'm not sure how that will look on my resume, but it's all such a fun journey into the fog of the unknown..

I'm starting to realize that the less my heart moves the heavier it gets, the more dust it collects, the less kindness I feel. But when I let my heart constantly stir like a cotton candy machine, the lighter and sweeter it becomes.

My relationship with the Great Mystery has turned into a wide-mouthed Wyoming river. Every bend is a new revelation. Sometimes the flow ebbs me into a comfortable eddy and other times it becomes rapid where my stomach ends up in my throat.

Just like a river is constantly evolving, my spirituality is always changing and becoming something new every day. It's said that we can't step into the same river twice. I find that sentiment to be true when it comes to my connection with God. Every day the Divine changes forms to meet me where I am at. Every day the Great Love invites me to enter the flow as we explore Wonderland together one river bend at a time together.

To live as moving water - to flow from one natural wonder to the next - is how I want to spend the rest on days left with Creation. To be a part of the flow of this wonderful mystic adventure of existence.

So, now, I wish I could go back in time and answer the question that hundreds of adults asked me when I was growing up.

I think I would answer it a bit differently.

"John, what do you want to do when you grow up?"

"I want to become a river. I want to flow into wonder."

Wonder *Wilds*

when the church I was sitting in became just another building to me
- I tore down my own walls and stopped locking all of my doors

until the altars became sunflowers
and the narrow pews turned into wide streams

now

my favorite places to pray
are spots where the divine has
traded in precise architecture
for a bit of untamed anarchy

like in the wilds of my heart

~ it's the unexplored expanse inside of me - where God asks me the most beautiful
questions while we both lay hands on each of the trees we walk past

yes, my love, my faith has lost some of its form - I'm like a tiny cloud that broke
away from the great thunderstorm

my faith surrendered so much of the structure I used to require - but now my soul
has never felt more deeply rooted in the humming mantle, below our feet

yes, my love, this is why I smell like pine needles when I come back from praying

once the walls fell down
I found so much wonder

that it causes me to ache
in all the most lovely ways

Wonder*Glow*

Absorb as much of the light
 as you can whenever it falls on you

~so that later

when you are lost
in the midnight
of your darkest despair

your tears will
glow in the dark
like fireflies

and we will be able to
follow the glow
    to come rescue you

my love,
I swear

   ~ I will find you

Wonder*Bubbles*

when I think about creation I often imagine God as a small child

wildly blowing
glowing bubbles
into the very
first darkness

these beaming orbs;

dancing and whirling
with delight into the
now dimly lit expanse

they are like children released
for an endless summer vacation

~ untethered and exploring

everything is
waiting for them

I can see it so clear,

these trembling newborn
radiant bubbles are everywhere now

some bubbles popping like
wedding fireworks

some bubbles
kissing each other so
madly that the skin between
then opens up and they

become a lovestruck galaxy

some bubbles
are hovering
In place

some are spinning
like Kerosine pool balls

some rocketing off into
the unfolding distance
to chase the fringe
of infinity

I wish you could
see what I see

it's all such a joyful chaos

and with every beat
of God's infectious laughter
these blazing bubbles ignite
even more

and it doesn't
take long for
the universe
to come alive

like a field of
blazing sunflowers

and I can smell
the sweet aroma
of an endless spring

I don't know much

about science

and even less about God

but I really believe
the creation story
has to be centered
around a child at play

~it just has to be

Wonder*Heart*

the places in our heart
where the world took bites
out of us

may never fully heal
  and will likely become
wide open spaces

> *~ be careful to not fill them*
> *with just anything or anyone*

your wounds aren't supposed
to become attics for you to hoard
unnecessary junk

these holes in our hearts
are holy sites
and we should treat
 them as such

so when visiting your old wounds
make sure to take your shoes off
and turn off your cell phone

sit by candlelight
  and watch how the shadows

tell the story how brave you are

                        ~ to survive

Wonder*Dawn*

I cried at dawn because I know I'll
never see this same sky ever again

with this exact
cloud formations

or the speckled pattern
of birds flirting with
the yawning horizon

how could I not weep?

**how can I not live in a
state of constant wonder***ment***?**

Wonder *Wander* One

I took a wrong turn
on my way to become
the person the world
expected me to be

and now I am wandering in
the deep wilds of my heart

I can't find
the path I was
once on

because I'm constantly being
distracted by the unexpected joy of
not knowing what new little lake
or sprawling cave that I will bump
into next

I'm too busy looking
for psalms that have been
written in moss on the
tree trunks inside of me
or mysterious rock formations
that radiate an ancient energy

to spend any of my time
sending out signal flares
for a search party to come
and find me

my love,
yes, I'm really lost

but

much to
my surprise

~ I don't want to be found

every step forward
leads me to a new undiscovered
land inside of me

my curiosity has become the compass
that keeps inviting me on
to continue my journey inward

it would be so easy to
stop and wait for rescue

so I could return to
the safe path
that only leads
to death's well-lit
and comfortable
waiting room

but my love,

maybe there is nothing
safe about being on
the well trodden
that path I had been
on my whole life

maybe there is nothing
comfortable about
just passing our time acting
like everybody else

maybe we were
created to constantly
surprise ourselves
by exploring every acre
of the natural creation
inside of us

maybe we are born
to get a bit lost

there are so many
hidden waterfalls inside of us
just waiting for us
to stand naked under

if we just put down
the map for a bit

and walk into the backcountry
of our hearts

we will be amazed what
wonders we will find

my love,

please don't fear
wandering
away from the path
you've been on
your whole life

and into the expanse
of what the Great Love
has in store for you

we didn't fight
to be exist
just to be on a
luxury cruise

life is meant to be a
once-in-a-lifetime odyssey
of discovery and adventure

and remember,
when we don't
know the way back
to our old home

the unknown can become
our new home

and we can build it
we can build it
we can build it
we can build our new home together

one step

one revelation

one step

one miracle

one step

one marvel

one step at a time

Wonder*Portrait*

A photo taken in 2022 by the new James Webb Telescope of our amazing universe was described by NASA Administrator Bill Nelson in the following way:

"If you held a grain of sand on the tip of your finger at arm's length, that is the part of the universe that you're seeing [in this image] — just one little speck of the universe."

Of course I had to write a poem about it...

*this single grain of cosmic sand
contains infinite wonder*

*this little speck of an unfolding universe
is packed to the rim with miracle*

*this snapshot in time
recites a gospel
of relentless creation
that tells the story of
a master artist who
refused to paint by
numbers and without
a single inhibition*

*this image is proof
that the gift of life
is beyond anything
we can possibly imagine*

*this photo is the park bench
where science and spirit can
meet and listen to one another*

yes, the vastness of
of our existence that
has no borders
or shorelines where the waves
of creation brush up against

~ it is endless

but don't let that make you
feel small

because every particle of light
that exists in this sprawling picture is just
as important as the light in your eyes

you were formed by the same
breath of energy that can stretch
light from across the cosmos right
to the front porch of our soul

my love,

we all came from the same
celestial mixing bowl

this is our family picture

this is us

Wonder *Worm*

Earthworm: Um? Good morning.

Me: Oh, morning. Did I wake you?

Earthworm: Well, yes. You were crying and your big tears sorted of flooded me out of my bed I made out of leaves.

Me: Yikes, sorry. I'm kind of going through it right now.

Earthworm: I understand. I was almost eaten by a robin yesterday. Really close call. Really scary.

Me: This storm I'm in is going to destroy me.

Earthworm: I know that it's easy to feel that way but I have learned that all storms end. Even the really scary ones.

Me: What's the point of surviving if I feel like I don't matter to this world. I'm too insignificant.

Earthworm: Whenever I think that way I just get to work on feeding the earth right around me. Maybe I can't change the whole world - but I can make this little patch of soil I'm digging in a better place.

Me: I am too exhausted to do anything.

Earthworm: That's just despair talking. Do what I do.

Me: What's that?

Earthworm: Wiggle your butt and get to work.

Me: You want me to wiggle my butt?

Earthworm: 🎵 Just a little bit 🎵

Me: No.

Earthworm: Come on. You'll feel better.

Me: Feel better? The only thing I feel is helpless!

Earthworm: You're not helpless. There's something you can do right now to not feel so helpless.

Me: What can I do?

Earthworm: You can be a helper.

Wonder *Wind*

I used to hate the wind
but now I kind of love it

because someday

I'm going to be
a part of the breeze

so are you

and someday

I'll find you again
you as we pass
through the same
pinetree

I think our souls
are part kite

and someday

we will get all
tangled up
together in the sky

maybe that is
why the world
seems windier
these days

there are so many
spirits holding on

to each other as
they reunite in mid air

and someday

I'll prove to you
that every gust
is just our beloveds
racing each other
to the next wind chime

oh, my love,

someday we will both
be part of the same flow

and we will be

together
together
together
again

Wonder*Doubt*

When I was 16 years old,
I heard Michael Stipe sing,

"I'm losing my religion,"

my heart started to stir
and simmer.

I didn't know that
losing a religion
was an option.

Catholicism was the
center of my universe,
the galaxy my world spun around.

I wondered:

> *what would happen*
> *if I lost my orbit*
> *to the faith my parents*
> *raised me in?*

> *where would I go if I started*
> *to drift into open space?*

Had I asked the wrong person at the time, I'm sure they would have said that a person who lost their faith would be a passenger on the bullet train straight to hellfire.

So, I buried that first pang of doubt
deep down in the mantle inside of me

and went on pretending that
I wasn't starting to lose my tether
to my Catholic upbringing.

But I was starting to feel like the sheep
who was starting to explore the outside
fringes of the herd I had been safely living
inside of for years and years.

It didn't help that I would often witness another trembling sheep get shamed and
silenced by a shepherd whenever they openly questioned the rules of the herd we
were in.

I remember when I was half my age,
I went into a box to confess my growing uncertainty.

The person on the other side of the veil
asked me why I was having a hard time
believing in what I had been taught about God for my entire life.

"I don't know," I answered honestly.

"That's not a good enough excuse for you to question your faith," the priest replied.
"If you are going to go down that road, you need more of a reason than 'I don't
know'."

I offered a half-assed rebuttal about
how not knowing why I had such doubts
was a perfectly okay place for me to be.

The man on the other side of the box was
not impressed and responded with a line
that I will never forget:

"You know who loves your answer? The devil."

"Oh, I am pretty sure there isn't an actual devil," I replied without thinking.

I immediately wished I hadn't, as the priest went on for about twenty minutes
about the power of evil and encouraged me to read more C.S. Lewis.

It was how I learned that it would make
 things easier to just keep my doubts to myself

and to quit going to confession.

So, I went on pretending the great pretend of being a good Catholic.

Yet year after year,

I found the grip I had on my faith
(or maybe it was the grip it had on me)
get looser and looser.

And before I knew it, those
doubts I buried deep inside
of me became mountain ranges,

and the happy plains of my
Catholicism became towering peaks
of sharp questions that I wanted to explore.

Suddenly, like a frog in boiling water,
the realization of what was happening to me was too late.

I had lost my religion.

I was Michael Stipe,
I was a runaway galaxy,
I was a lost sheep.

Now I have made my home
inside the bend of a question mark
as I look at my existence and this
miracle we all find ourselves in with new eyes.

Maybe someday all these doubts
and curiosities of mine will lead
me back to where I started among
the precise cobblestone streets
of the faith I was born into.

Or perhaps I will end up
living among the wild trees
and howling wolves of mystery.

I really don't know where I will end up,
and that is a perfectly okay place to be
right now,

and maybe it will be
for the rest of my life

how exciting is that?!

Wonder*Dreams*

My love, here is a lullaby for you.

In the sacred space that exists between wake and Dreamland is a place where you can empty out the pockets of your heart of all the fear and worry you picked up during the day. Let go of your anxieties before you slip under the curtain of the mystic realm.

If you really need all of your frets and worries you will be allowed to grab them again at dawn. My guess is most of them aren't needed.

> For tonight - enter sleep with a heart so light that you
> may have the chance to drift up past the stars.

I love you.

Wonder*Angels*

I used to get so bored
with being alive

> then one day I started to pretend
> that I was an angel who was
> sent to Earth on a secret mission to
> absorb as much beauty as I could
> before being called back home

> then a couple days later, I started to pretend that
> everyone else was on the exact same mission that I was on:

> *to gather beauty, like me*

then soon after,
I stopped pretending altogether

> And now

I see halos EVERYWHERE I go

Wonder*Kind*

God dried her tears and waited for the next
brand new soul to enter the departure room.

The Divine drew a slow, deep breath. Time stopped for a moment and then raced
to catch up. The door between time and space opened, and a little purple cloud
floated in timidly.

God met it with a big smile.

 "There you are, little soul!
 I've been waiting an eternity for this moment!"
 God said with her trademarked laugh.

"Here I am..." the new soul said with a shaky voice.

 "Are you ready for your first day?" God asked.

The new soul approached the tube and nodded tentatively. It studied the tube
that was supposed to send it down to Earth in a flurry of light and song.

 *"Don't be nervous, little one," God said while cupping the soul up in her large
hands*
 and holding it tight up against her luminous naked chest.

 "The journey to your body will be smooth.
 It will feel like riding a tide."

"I don't know what a tide is..."

 "Oh, you will someday, little one, you will!" God exclaimed with a chuckle.
 "Tides are amazing! If you ever want to remember where you came from,
 go spend time watching waves."

"Okay..." the new soul said.

God's smile widened. She loved this part. God held the soul even closer.

"Ready?"

"Okay..." the new soul replied.

The warmth of God's touch spread a charge through its wispy form, like the softest of lightning.

"Before you go, I need to ask you the question that I ask every single soul I send to Earth,"
God said while laying the soul down into the tube.

"All right..." the new soul responded weakly.

God leaned down and kissed the new soul at the apex of its billowing shape. The kiss sent another charge of electricity through the soul—this one much stronger than the first. The new soul felt the first pangs of life move through it.

Its essence groaned with creation. The tube began to hum. An ancient song began to play.

"Are you ready for your question, little soul?" God asked.

"Yes..." the soul replied.

God stared straight into the core of the soul with the gentlest of eyes. Her eyes contained the light of Genesis.

God leaned in and asked:

"Will you be kind to every other soul you meet while you are in your body on Earth?"

The soul paused a bit before answering—for dramatic effect.

This question wasn't a surprise. The new soul had been told during orientation that God would ask it—but wanted to pretend to give a thoughtful reply. The new soul wanted God to think that it had reflected on it deeply despite the fact that there was only one way it could answer the question.

After a moment the new soul answered:

"Yes, God, of course, I'll be kind."

"To every other soul?"

"Yes—to every other soul."

God's smile stretched out into the corners of the universe.

"Well then, little love, your adventure begins right now!
Enjoy the adventure!"

The new soul began to vibrate. The tube closed around it, and in a flash it was gone.

"Have a great first day on Earth, little one. Remember to look for the waves if you ever get homesick down there!" God yelled out to the fading contrails of the freshly vanished soul.

The room fell silent.
God began to sob.

"Why are you crying?" an eavesdropping Nebula asked as it was passing by.

"Because the new souls always unintentionally lie when they answer my question,"
God said while brushing the tears from her burning cheeks.

"They aren't going to be kind?" the Nebula inquired.

"Not to everyone," God replied quietly. *"It's really hard for them down there to live with kindness. They eventually decide that it's fine to only show empathy to*

certain people. Sometimes they will only be kind in order to get something out of it. They treat kindness as a transaction."

The purple nebula frowned.

"They forget the promise they made..." God said with her voice trailing off.

"If you know that these new souls are going to forget about their promise to you, why do you even bother sending them down there in the first place?" the Passing Nebula asked.

"Just in case," God whispered.

"Just in case, what?" the aspiring constellation replied.

"Just in case they remember."

The nebula hugged God farewell before disappearing into itself.

God drew a slow, deep breath. Time stopped for a moment and then raced to catch up.

God dried her tears and waited for the next brand new soul to enter the departure room.
The door between time and space opened, and a little aqua cloud floated in timidly.

God met it with a big smile.

"There you are, little soul!
I've been waiting an eternity for this moment!"
God said with her trademarked laugh.

Wonder*Kisses*

I was a teenager camp counselor
sitting in a scalding hot tub at midnight
with as many other teenage
camp counselors as we could pack in

without a single adult in sight

about thirteen puberty-ravaged
caught in the uncomfortable purgatory
that exists between childhood and maturation

we were a baker's dozen
of pre-ripened strawberries
waiting for Mister Time to speed up
the clock inside our bodies so we
could bloom under a late July sunburst

there we were
in our very own
churning hot tub
of awkward
teenage glances
and flushed cheeks

~six boys
~six girls

one me

and a sea of raging
hormones between us all

everybody flirting with each
other like it was their last
night on earth

except me—my girlfriend (and future wife) was back at home and I barely had
enough courage to romance her, let alone anybody new

the six boys six girls
focused on the games taking place
under the rolling water

legs tangled together
fingers finding fingers
thighs pressed to thighs

~lips longing to be locked into
someone else's lips like legos

an unrehearsed performance
of synchronized wooing

by giggling under-age Olympians striving
to earn the gold medals of their first
real kiss with tongue

the night stretched on,
into deep morning

~six brides
~for six brothers
one me

and a field of stars sliding
across the sky
overhead

while the group vamped
and courted with each other

I set my eyes to the
endless universe above

and for the first time imagined what
infinity would feel like

what would it be like to fall into forever?
to never end?
to have an endless story?
to never be afraid to die?

the great beyond was a mystery to me

while at the same time the winking universe
stared down below at the overfilled hot tub of teenage lovers

the universe was nestled;

contemplating what a true love's kiss would taste like?

wondering what it would be like to fall in love with somebody else?

how would it feel to hear somebody whisper with hot breath in its ear?

to the great beyond, we were as
much of a mystery to it as it
was to us

the sun started to wake up
and the universe began to hide its ornaments
and the hot tub gang began to clear out

everybody going back to
catch a few hours of sleep

I lingered a bit longer
in the roiling boil of
the hot tub

it was
just the fading
night sky and I

two aliens reflecting on
the nature of their counterpart

a sleepy teenager
&
the vanishing universe

~both a bit jealous of the other

**under the growing daybreak
light of a fresh tangerine sun**

Wonder*Cradle*

when you fall

  you don't always
have to bounce
right back up again

you're a human
- not a ball

my love,

the next time you fall
down hard

allow the crater you created
to become a cradle

~ take a deep breath

         and rest,
         my love,

                            just rest

rest

                            rest

         rest

Wonder*Commandment*

~ a spiritualist told me that
I'll live a thousand different lives
~a scientist explained that
I'll just get one run here on *Earth*

~ an angry preacher offered that
I'll burn if I don't see things their way
~ a sleepy hippie claimed that
I've been so loved since my *birth*

~ a skeptic will tell me over drinks that
God does not exist
~ while a faithful disciple will claim that
God is simply taking a *nap*

~ some folks are trying to sell me
on their exact path to heaven
~ some are desperately imploring me
to set fire to any given *map*

~ I don't understand much about
this great mystery we're all in
~ as I haven't found one answer
that will ever quite *work*

~ so, I'll just be here following
my own spiritual path
~ whose only theology states
"thou shall not be a *jerk*"

John Roedel

Wonder*Warm*

my love, when you
feel all alone

go outside and
sit under the sun

let it *hold* you like a *baby*
let it *warm* you like a *seed*
let it *dry* your tears like a *healer*

no matter what happens to you next

you will *always*
be loved

by the light

Wonder*Doors*

God kept losing my phone number
~ and my friend, the Holy Spirit went full *ghost*.
Buddha was on a paid sabbatical in space
while Jesus sold bracelets on the other *coast*.

I have cried in a pew for some answers—
I screamed into the sky for a bit of *relief*.
There was flood water rising in my Ark
as my questions lost all of their baby *teeth*.

The great mystery had become an introvert,
hiding behind a twice-bombed-out *church*.
I craned my neck for angels riding doves
but found no rescue for my endless *search*.

My faith life was sent to a dingy hospice care unit,
diagnosed with a case of recurring *doubt*.
Turns out the afterlife housing I applied for
had a tricky HOA and no room for my *drought*.

I sat patiently for God's receptionist
to call my name, like waiting at an abandoned bus *stop*.
So, I put on my shoes and started wandering
instead of waiting for the new divine map to *drop*.

Now I walk without a GPS to show me the way—
I see clues of the Great Love out in the *wild*,
written for me in the clouds and on tree bark
whenever I look with the wide eyes of a *child*.

In a universe packed full of newborn yawning stars,
where I am a particle on a particle of *sand*,

I feel seen by God as I chase every fluttering wonder
and allow my heart to billow and *expand*.

I treated the Divine like an official ATM,
where I put in my pin to receive my "good boy" *pay*.
Now, God answers me with moonbeams at night
or a kiss from my wife at the start of the *day*.

I can't find Creation in fancy places with high ceilings—
I discover Grace easier on the *cheap*.
On Sunday mornings, I'll be listening
to silent wildflower sermons with the other lost *sheep*.

Every doubt is an open window to a foreign land,
and curiosity is a question mark-shaped open *door*.
**There is so much wonder to discover about God
as we give ourselves the freedom to *explore*.**

Wonder_Listeners_

someday we will all be sitting

around the campfire together

taking turns sharing

the epic story of our lives

"I understand you," we say to the storyteller

when they are finished

after everyone has a chance to speak

then we turn to our neighbor

and run our thumbs across

the scars we each brought in

and they smudge right off of us

as if they were Lenten ashes

and the fire rises

and the music between us grows

and we start to dance

and we are no longer strangers

we are a cracking

campfire community

of seekers and healers

~ where the act of listening to our neighbor

share their story is a sacrament

~ where saying "I hear you" is

the most powerful prayer we can ever utter

□□

and we keep saying it over and over

and over and over to each other

until the dawn comes

and the fire turns into smoke

as we turn into a flock of morning birds

~ who travel the world together as a murmuration

Wonder*Orbs*

There are so many stories of people who describe a brilliant "tunnel of light" they pass through during a near-death experience. They often report that they travel upward/inward/outward through this beautiful tunnel until they reach the next place.

Those who have had this experience sometimes add that along their journey through this lovely passage of light, they bump into their deceased loved ones for a quiet and often thoughtful reunion.

I doubt I've earned an experience that is quite so opulent.

Let that tunnel be for the saints.
Let that tunnel be for those who have buildings named after them.
Let that tunnel be for those who aced every exam given to them.
Let that tunnel be for the queens and kings of industry.
Let that tunnel be for those who never missed Sunday church.
Let that tunnel be for people who never screamed at God.
Let that tunnel be for those who refused to doubt their own heart.

Let that tunnel be reserved for those who expect
or need to see it after they shed their skin.

I don't.

I think my journey into forever wonderment will have a lot less frills to it. At best, my afterlife orientation will be considered "the basic package."

When I die I won't be marching down the divine's red carpet answering questions from paparazzi angels asking me what I'm wearing.

When I go, I'm certain that I'll be entering the hereafter through a side door and not the grand lobby.

Instead of passing through a shimmering tunnel, I'll find myself on a woodland path just after sunset.

The trail will be marked with a series of small votive candles, like the ones you buy in bulk at the dollar store. The candlelight will be low-lit as each flame barely flickers right above the pool of growing melted wax below.

It will be so quiet that even though I'll be walking on dead leaves, they won't crinkle.

The only noise that I'll hear comes from the two dozen (or so) little soft pink glowing orbs that float in the trees about 10 to 15 yards away from where I stand on the path.

The orbs hum a melody that I've never heard before but instantly recognize.

I follow the candles down the path as their light casts my shadow against the backdrop of the thousands of trees that encircle me.

The strange thing is that whenever I look at it, my shadow always looks like a jellyfish swimming through deep water.

After walking (swimming?) for an hour, or maybe it's a month, that could actually be a decade.

The candles eventually lead me to a small cabin that rests between two towering redwood trees that stretch so far into the clouds above that I can't see the tops of them.

- The wooden cabin door has my name carved on it.

- When I open it, I find a really comfy spot.

- A small kitchen with all of my favorite snacks and comfort soups loaded in the shelves.

- It looks like I'll be here for a long visit.

- On the counter, some exotic wildflowers sit in a tall vase.

- The flowers have alternating colors for each petal.

- I notice that the flowers sway back and forth in rhythm, dancing to a song I cannot quite hear.

- There is an oversized glass of royal blue liquid that tastes like the freshest water I have ever drunk - and every time I take a sip, the glass refills itself.

- The more I drink, the more my skin starts to turn into a swirl of colors.

- The more I drink, the more my body starts to look like a hurricane on Jupiter.

- There is a crackling fireplace that I somehow know was lit for me on the day I was created a couple thousand ages ago.

- There is a cozy bed in the corner of the cabin that has my old childhood blanket folded on the center of it.

- It is such a soft blanket that has so many little yellow and white ducks woven in it.

- I used to love this blanket so much - maybe too much that my parents eventually had to hide it from me.

- I walk over to the table, and there is a note written in pencil that reads:

Welcome home, you must be exhausted from your travels. Rest, my love, rest for as long as you need to. When you are ready, go out to the trees. Pick one of them and place your hands on it. Then wait for what happens next. Do this for every single tree in the forest. Visit each of them.

I love you,

First Light.

I peek out the windows of the cabin and look out into the woods that encircle me. There are so many trees, and I start to worry that visiting each of them will take forever. I worry that I might never be able to leave this place.

I can see the pink orbs looking back at me from the edge of the wild, bobbing up and down while moving side to side in the same patterns as the flowers that were waiting for me in the cabin.

Suddenly, I become so tired.

- I lie down on the bed and pull my old blanket up against my bare chest.

- I drift off into a sleep so deep, I feel like I am as old as the sun when I wake up.

- I forgot to shut the door before my long slumber, and I notice that a couple of the orbs have made their way into my cabin.

- I sit up in bed as the orbs come to wrap themselves around my hand and start to gently tug on me like a child taking an adult into a waterpark.

- Soon, these two orbs draw me outside into the forest.

- It isn't dark anymore; it's daybreak.

- But instead of a single blazing sun above me, there are four gentler stars.

- Each of them has various shades of purple, from violet to Lenten.

- I am guided to stand in front of a small tree that grows about 20 feet away from my cabin door.

- The orbs place my hands on the tree, and immediately I feel like I am plugged into an outlet.

- A tickling electricity passes through me.

- Suddenly, I fall into a memory of my time on Earth that I had forgotten all about.

- A memory that I accidentally buried under a couple thousand unimportant pages of my story:

It's a memory of where I stood with my beloved as we kissed under a shower of sprinklers in a park where we swore our love for each other when we were teenagers. The water feels so cold, but her lips are warm, like twin sunbeams cutting through a freezing winter afternoon.

I watch as, between clumsy kisses, the two of us unintentionally conduct a ceremony that binds our hearts together while we are together on Earth. It is hard to explain how I watch myself from above while still being in my body while this memory plays out.

This is one of the great mysteries of the great beyond, I suppose.

I can feel the wave of new love flow through my old soul, like it is happening all over again.

Maybe it is.

Some memories contain more energy than others, an energy that ignites a sleeping caldera inside us, even while we wander in the hereafter.

"Oh, how I love you," my spirit whispers to the memory of my lover.

The sweet memory fades in the most peculiar way. The tree I touch begins to fold into itself, its bark softening and curling inward, transforming into another radiant pink orb. I still taste my beloved's lip gloss on my lips. I feel the heat of her touch still.

The memory grows inside me like a flower.

I will carry it with me wherever I go from now on.

The new orb floats beside me, bobbing up and down, slowly moving side to side. The orb joins the other two that first led me outside the cabin, guiding me to the next tree.

This particular tree has a twisted trunk, its branches stripped bare. I place my hands on the wood, and once again I fall into a memory, this one far less pleasant.

I'm in my 20s, with a whiskey drink in my hand, surrounded by a slew of my buddies.

I smell the smoke and taste my burning ego in the back of my throat. There is another young man sitting across from me at a bar table. He doesn't fit in with us, and I do my best to let him know it.

Every time he speaks, I grab his words like balloons, twisting them up and throwing each one back in his face. My quick wit and shadow put him on trial for the crime of not being like the rest of us. I convict him easily in front of a jury of my laughing peers.

A chill passes over me, colder than regret. It's shame. I am horrified of this version of myself who treated another's heart like a playground.

"I'm so sorry..." my observing self whispers to the young man I tormented.

With that, the tree folds itself up into another pink orb. The smell of the dank bar rests in my nostrils, as does the pang of guilt I feel for how terrible I was to that poor man.

The memory grows inside me like a flower.
I will carry it with me wherever I go from now on.

I look up at all the trees that encircle me, and I immediately know the work ahead of me. Each tree is a memory of my time being alive on Earth, and I must spend time with each one of them to release them.

I stand at a crossroads, a decision to make: to visit each memory, to explore other trees, each one a chapter of my life.

The orbs hum softly around me, a chorus of past lives and lessons learned

I take a deep breath, and I get to work. I don't know how many years I will spend releasing each memory

The good ones, the passionate ones, the heartbreaking ones, the shameful ones. All of them become pink orbs

I go inside the cabin from time to time to rest, drink the blue water, and eat soup. Exploring our stories in such a manner, it turns out, can be quite exhausting

Over the course of my work, the forest begins to disappear

Eventually, I am encircled by only soft pink glowing orbs that gently bob up and down and move slowly from side to side as they follow me around the woodland of my memories

After visiting the last tree, featuring the only time I remember my mom kissing my forehead,

I watch as the final orb rises out of my memory

All the orbs begin to swirl and melt into each other in the most brilliant light show I have ever seen. After a bit of theatrics, these orbs join to become a beaming passage. My smile stretches out over an entire galaxy as I stand in front of a tunnel of light.

I am as surprised as anyone to find out that I have my own tunnel. With all the memories growing inside me, and all the lessons I have learned, the love I shared, the mistakes, the failures, the kisses, the sunsets I experienced,

they all come with me as I walk through the tunnel of pink orbs and into the adventure of what comes next

Wonder*Friend*

Dear You,

I think it's time for you to make friends
with the thoughts in your head.
If you find that you are unable to do
that, then I suggest

**you start thinking
the kind of thoughts that
are worthy of your friendship.**

Wonder*Skin*

my love,

don't let your
skin become
so thick that
nothing can
hurt you anymore

getting wounded
is part of the experience

the scars you
collect are all
part of your story

take off your armor
and give vulnerability
a chance to paint
your naked form

feel the sunlight
on your shoulders

let the wind move
through your hair

give your tears a
chance to be counted

allow us to be swept
up in your smile

~ you see, my love,

you weren't born
to be hidden behind
a towering wall

you were formed out
of an ancient whisper to
become a natural wonder
where we all visit to
listen to the songbirds
sing through the pines of
your evergreen beauty

you were given this skin
to be kissed softly
 - don't let it grow scales

you were given your eyes
to reflect starlight
- don't close them to keep us from
seeing your soul

you were given your hands
to lace inside another hand
- don't keep them constantly
folded in your lap

my love,

I know this world
can be a sharpened spear
that will often pierce you

but

when given a choice
bleeding is always

better than apathy

someday when we
meet in the moving
cosmic river that exists
on the crawling fringe
of everything

let's take turns
washing each other's
scars while saying
the same prayer
over and over:

"I got this wound
for caring and I
got this one for
having an open heart

but that is the cost
that comes from being
a work of sacred art."

Wonder*Prayer*

I've become so exhausted
from praying

and then waiting
                    and waiting
                                and waiting

and then nothing happens

prayer is too
one-sided
for me

it's like trying
to be pen pals
with Saturn

I have been unsuccessfully begging
God to notice me for years

so, I've stopped trying to
coerce the great mystery
to arrange my life the way I
want it to be or to remove a
tumor from my friend

instead of praying into
a holy silence

I flirt with the unfolding rave
that exists all around me

now I just listen to

the wild grass grow

  and smell raindrops
sunbathing on clouds

and feel July sunbeams
roll down my skin like
hot raw honey

and taste the sea salt
on my lips whenever
I watch the ocean dance

I have quit asking
the unseen to see me

Instead, I've become
a better witness to
the untamed wonder
that has been begging
for me to pay attention
to it for years

because maybe
Creation and I
have been too busy
speaking

to actually hear
each other

I'll be quiet first, God,

so I can listen to Your
howl move through
the trees and
           the holes in my heart

then maybe if You
take a breath

I'll get a turn to talk
in order for You
to finally hear me

but even if I don't

at least I'll have
heard a symphony

perhaps prayer isn't
telephone call
with a formal King

it's a river trip
with an eternal poet

**who writes love letters
to us in the water**

Wonder*Body*

Every morning I have a blind date
with my body - and as I do,

a million questions
run through my head.

Who is this person
sitting across from
me in the mirror?

Am I my own soulmate?

Are the dreams in my heart
and my thoughts in my head
perfect strangers?

How can I open my soul
to this imperfect human
who is staring back at me?

How can I learn to love
their wrinkles?

How can I build a
future with this person?

And every morning
during my blind date
with my own image,

I remember the secret
to any great relationship:

It is to let them see you
as you really are.

~ So, how do I see myself?

As a piece of cosmic art,
or as a half-shattered bowl?

Maybe it's both things
at the same time.

My love,

In order to feel at home
in your skin,

you must learn to
be yourself
with yourself,

and to see the beauty
in yourself
when you look at yourself.

All first dates
are awkward.

     ~ So be patient with yourself

as you get to know the person,
in the mirror.

Don't let them slip
through your fingers,

because, because, because—

     ~ they are the love of your life.

Wonder*Church*

Lately, when I need to pray,

I go to the church that
has no doors,

and where the walls are
made of carved granite.

I sit under its moving roof
on a pew that smells
like fresh pine,

and fold my hands quietly
until God joins me. ~

Here in this most ancient of churches,
I watch a dozen fat rainbow angels dressed
as trout dance in the baptismal font

and wonder out loud:

"When will I too,
be made anew?"

There is a special kind of holy quiet here
that rings much louder than any fat
church bell I have ever known,

and the silence often rattles my ribs. ~

Its choir loft is high up in a bird's nest,
and its confessional is a breeze
that asks me to speak my sins,

and I do, and then they are carried away. ~

The longer I sing psalms in this church,
the shorter my memory for all of
my past mistakes become.

And that is when I hear
the Voice of Love speak:

> *"Oh tired light, oh wounded heart,*
> *oh my child of crumbling grace,*
> *come plant your feet in this Eden,*
> *come rest in this sacred space.*
>
> *Oh weary traveler, oh somber fire,*
> *oh shaking heart that is prone to fear,*
> *come lay in My ribboned water,*
> *come to fully know that I'm right here.*
>
> *Oh wilting daisy, oh dying star,*
> *oh broken song that needs a name,*
> *come sit with Me among the wild,*
> *and then you'll never be the same."*

God and I take turns
saying all we need to say
to each other.

I speak in short, heavy, jagged breaths,
and the Divine replies in thin, long pauses.

This goes on until the sun begins to set. ~

That's when it's time to leave,
and even though I go home,
I'm always still there

in the antiquated church
of trees and valleys,

where foxes are lectors,
where horizons are steeples,
where clouds are vestibules,
where campfires are incense,
where time is a gospel,
where the great flow is a sacrament,
where forests are community.

Where a little piece of me always still remains,
talking to the voice of whispering Love,
as I watch trout be slain in the spirit,

and I can't stop marveling
at the altar of creation.

Wonder*Maybe*

-maybe we are here to teach each other how to love

- maybe Earth is a classroom and we are to take turns being students and professors

        - maybe we need to quit grading each other so harshly

        - maybe the only homework assignment we have been given is solving the equation of kindness

        - maybe empathy is a "study abroad" program where we spend time in the foreign hearts of strangers

        - maybe forgiveness is the final exam

        - maybe we are never meant to graduate and remain forever students of how to love and care for each other.

oh, just maybe

Wonder*Psalm*

Come peace wave
Come hope star
Come healing rain
Come singing scar

Come opening doors
Come fading pain
Come kinder eyes
Come unlocked chains

Come velvet sermon
Come forgiven sin
Come abandoned rifle
Come rainbow skin

Come holy mystery
Come messy art
Come lingering kisses
Come untamed heart

Come night swimming
Come morning mist
Come winter melt
Come unclenched fist

Come garden chapels
Come righted wrongs
Come angel feathers
Come campfire songs

Come comfy socks
Come selfless love
Come dancing moon

Come Exodus dove

Come shouted pardons
Come silenced shame
Come mercy ledger
Come restored name

Come hilltop picnics
Come backyard wakes
Come swearing unicorns
Come saintly snakes

Come slow romance
Come fast heartache
Come hospice promises
Come endless daybreak

Come clean oceans
Come crystal streams
Come secret wishes
Come captured dreams

Come hurricane eye
Come volcano veins
Come forest lungs
Come universe brain

Come courageous doubt
Come honey wine
Come unwritten gospels
Come unmistakable sign

Come fresh starts
Come letting go
Come easy days
Come healing woe

Come violin tongue
Come piano breath
Come musical soul
Come ego death

Come strange questions
Come stranger replies
Come elderly stories
Come newborn cries

Come rebuilt bridges
Come listening ears
Come uncharted adventure
Come virgin frontiers

Come dragon courage
Come dolphin mind
Come explored dungeon
Come mountain climbed

Come gentle pillow
Come restful sleep
Come giggle tears
Come joyful weep

Come rushing spirit
Come sacred breeze
Come budding branches
Come chanting trees

Come compassion currency
Come forgiveness note
Come softer politics
Come peaceful votes

Come comet tails
Come ancient lights

Come cosmic energy
Come starry nights

Come weightless bibles
Come guiltless verses
Come sleeping dogma
Come unwalled churches

Come releasing past
Come moving on
Come self reconciliation
Come sweetest psalm

Come new chapter
Come morning dew
Come another chance

Come life renewed

Wonder*Search*

Dear Seeker,

Don't give up on your search
for the extraordinary.

It's everywhere. Everywhere. Everywhere.

The extraordinary is in your wrinkles and in the soil,
and in the buzz of a bee, in the smell of rain
and the taste of salt on your sweet lips.

My love,

*Marvel at the mundane
until it becomes a miracle.*

Become a detective who follows the clues
and breadcrumbs left by creation that lead
to a lovely new land for you to discover called

wonderment

Wonder *Theology*

I'm a conditional atheist

God does not exist for me on
the tip of a sharpened sword

or on the lips of a sermonizing
hate-evangelist who is foaming at the mouth

or in the licking flames of a torch held
by a marching bigot

or in any dogma that have been soaked in the ancient poison of guilt and self-
shame

the divine doesn't
exist for me anywhere
where wounds are being
caused in its name

I don't know about
how any of this works
but I've never found
much of God in the towering
hierarchy of unchecked power

the Great Mystery isn't a cracking whip
or a flag or an internet manifesto
or a pointed finger or a political party
or a dividing line or a box of ammo
or a corvette driven by a tv preacher
or a specific gender or a book bonfire

Creation is more of a florist

than she is a fundamentalist

the Weaver of Life is more interested
in stitching us together into a quilt
than how to separate us into metal bins

to come into relationship
with Unending Love shouldn't
require us to loathe ourselves

~ it should be the exact opposite

to know ourselves
is to know God

to love ourselves
is to love God

my love,

I believe that the divine
is just about everywhere

~ except in the slow-poison
sands of fear and control
where so many have built temples
for us to worship inside

~ in those places
I am an atheist

but everywhere else

there is so much
fertile soil

where we can let the sunflowers

of empathy grow wildly in
the spaces between us

and I've heard
that if we remain still

and listen so very closely
these evangelizing sunflowers
will whisper to each of us
a secret we once knew while we
were cooking in the cosmic womb:

"We are all loved equally."

Wonder_Romance_

Is the day when your soul slips out of your skin
and rejoins the stars?

Probably not.

But just in case -
I need you to know how much I love you.

Oh, how I love you so.

**I will savor every
second with you**

Wonder*Awakening*

you are finally waking up
from your extended slumber

stretch out your bare body
against the bed sheets
of your slow boil spring

let your yawning heart
grow wildly inside you

~ *like a second Eden*
  ~ *like an untamed superbloom*

when you're ready
sit up from your
resting place

and stare down at your reflection
in the once frozen lake that you thawed
with your sun-soaked breath

look at yourself
with genesis eyes

remind yourself of how
lovely you are

and that
you are the wonder landscape
creation carefully painted
with tender brushstrokes

and the deepest of sighs

wake,
 my love,

wake wake wake

your soul seed
is ready to burst
through the topsoil

every valley
every forest
 every field
every mountain
 every acre

inside of
you is stirring

I know you can feel it

your season of
growth is here

lean in to your blooms
as they ache themselves
back to life

your lazy slumber is over

time to rise
and dig your
toes into the soft
 moss of this world

as you stand up
to smell the sunrise

as if it were a daisy

~ remember this,
my love,

you are a masterpiece
of creation

and the inevitable
season of your awakening
is finally here

don't sleep in
rise rise rise
wake wake wake

I can already hear
the earth groan
with delight below us

as you let your
heart grow wild

~ after such a long winter

WonderService

whenever I feel helpless
in this overwhelming world

I become a helper

oh, oh,
my love

on the days when it feels like
I have no power

I serve others
you see, whenever
I wash the world's feet

**my hands immediately
stop shaking**

Wonder *Train*

by the time I am done writing this poem
I'll be a little bit closer to death

maybe you're reading these words
after I've already boarded the train

or maybe I'm still here at the station
writing on the platform walls

my love,

please know that whether I'm lingering
or now just an echo of an echo

this is the perfect moment
to finally tell you something
very important:

~I'm not afraid anymore~

and that I'm so grateful that
we are here now together
in this weird little secret room
of words that exist beyond
the world's physical flow

where my transcribed heart and your eyes
get to hold each other for a moment

regardless if I'm still wearing skin or not I remain thankful for so many things

~ to have felt sunshine on my neck

~ to have tasted orange sherbet
~ to have been kissed fiercely
~ to have swam in clear water

and, my love, by the time you are
done reading this little poem

you will be a little bit closer to death too

so, quit waiting for
the perfect moment to
do what you need to do
~ this is that moment ~

you know it is
you know it is
you know it is

you don't have enough
time to be afraid anymore

I have found that fear want
to make us all procrastinators

the only thing
you have time left
to be

~ is grateful

you ask:
"grateful for what?"

my love, you tell me...
what are you thankful for?

but you
better hurry up
and say it out loud
because

I think I can hear the train coming

Wonder *Toes*

I wasted so much
of my life waiting
for the next shoe to drop

that missed out on
all of the miracles
happening around me

I suppose,
now that I'm older,
that's the reason

~ why I'm always barefoot

my love,

I'm no longer
standing frozen
in fear waiting for
the arrival of the dooms

**I'm spending my
remaining days
walking with naked toes
among the blooms**

Wonder *Wanderer* Two

oh my love, there are now over 8 billion
of us here who are wearing skin over
our shimmering stardust forms

and despite
the arrogance
of a few of our
fellow stardusters

none of us are
actually from here

this is not our home
this is not our home
this is not our home

my love, we are dandelions
that grew on this green lawn
only after our seeds
blew in on the breeze

where did we come from?

I can't really remember
- but I don't think that place
was our home either

and someday when these
costumes we are wearing
start to wrinkle and warp

our shimmering stardust
will spill out through our

fading skin

~ and we will become
cosmic seeds again

~ and the wind will take
us somewhere new

this is not our home
this is not our home
this is not our home

~maybe we will never
actually have a home

~maybe we are built
to keep wandering

~maybe we are here
to travel across the universe

~ maybe we are made to
see it all - every inch of creation

~maybe we are crafted
to be endless travelers

~maybe death is a
roadtrip across the cosmos

and if I get taken to the
next new world
by the breeze before you are

I'll scout a new location
where our roots can get
all tangled up together again

in the fertile purple alien soil

this is not my home
this is not my home
this is not my home

~ but you are, my love

no matter
where I go next

you are my home
you are my home
you are my home

Wonder*Hammocks*

a dozen angels have started living in
the holes in my wounded heart

> *they have put up*
> *hammocks and started*
> *planting roses*

last night they had a bonfire where
they burned a box of my oldest regrets
and plated drums until dawn appeared

these angels have made themselves
at home inside
of my imperfect heart

in hopes
that someday

I will do the same

Wonder*Kaleidoscope*

3:30 a.m. I've been up all night.

And now, I really can't sleep because I just learned
that a group of butterflies is called a kaleidoscope.

I'm overwhelmed by that word:

kaleidoscope.

I close my eyes and imagine I'm walking
through a thick forest. Every tree is filled with
dozens of broken-open chrysalises.

I walk into a clearing.
I can see them now.

~A swirl of fluttering colors.
~A breathing wave of change agents.

The sky above me is now a billowing canvas
of dancing droplets of sacred paint.

The sound of ten thousand hovering wings
announces the end of winter.

The reign of the
smothering gray is over.

The season of dancing
rainbows has officially begun.

The kaleidoscope is growing
as more and more specks of
color rise up to join the festival.

The kaleidoscope is kissing
every dead, black tree back to life.

I detect a hint
of maple in the air,

and I decide that must be
what resurrection smells like.

The kaleidoscope of butterflies
is transforming the frozen, foggy world
into a spinning prism of new life.

I open my eyes. It's now 4 a.m. I still can't sleep. How can I? I have a living
kaleidoscope inside me. They are kissing all my dead parts back to life. I can hear
them fluttering when I hold my breath. I've never felt so warm. There are so many
empty cocoons in me. I'm transforming. My skin is constantly shedding under a
pulsing beat of rainbow light shards.

I'm now a child of Spring,
and suddenly—just like that—

**I can taste
maple syrup on my lips.**

Wonder*Sun*

on the days when you
don't like yourself very much at all

go outside
and stand
in the sun

and let the light
kiss your bare skin

over and over and
over and over and
over and and over

until you finally remember

that you are worth
traveling across the cosmos for

WonderSpectacle

nothing in
life is ordinary

~ everything is a bit supernatural

don't let your time
slip by without
seeing the miracle
in every stitch of
this quilt we are
sitting on together
under this praying tree

~ look down

each blade of grass
has a song of survival

~ look up

every cloud is a
art teacher

~ look around

everyone who is alive
is candle

the cliffs are
Old Testament psalms

the oceans are
a new gospel

~ look within

every breath we take
is genesis

every breath we take
is revelation

every tear we create
is a baptism

every word we speak
is the holy wind

it's all extraordinary

from the speakers
in your veins blasting
your heart's bass guitar
riff just under your skin

to the black hole
a trillion light years
away that is humming
a lullaby to the stars
she is putting to bed

it's all a
supernatural spectacle

miracles are everywhere

- and my love,
just so you know...

~ you are one of my
favorite one

Wonder*Fall*

most of the holes
that I have fallen
down
down

                    down down down
                        down

                                            down down
                                             down

                                    down
                        down

                        D
                        O
                        W
                        N

                    down down
                    down down

into turned out
to be cocoons

they weren't tombs,
my love,

            they were wombs

Wonder*Form*

this isn't how I planned for
my life to look like," I whispered
under my breath as I walked to my car

"tell me about it,"
an eavesdropping cloud
replied to me from above

I looked up and watched
the cloud billow between looking
like a dove and an open hand

the cloud continued:

"I used to be a snowfield in Montana.
I used to be a dewdrop kiss on a lily.
I used to be a puddle in a parking lot.
I used to be a river in Mexico.
I used to be a glacier.
I used to be a waterfall mist in a jungle.
oh, I have been so many things."

"doesn't that make you sad?" I asked the cloud

"it used to - but not anymore," the cloud replied while wrapping herself around
me like a scarf. "I don't think either of us were created to stay the same form our
entire life."

"I'm not sure I can let go of my old life," I sighed.

"oh you simply must," the cloud whispered in my ear. "because once you release
what you used to be and embrace who you are meant to be now - something
amazing will happen," the cloud said

"what's that?" I asked while looking at my hands that were beginning to billow
and shapeshift.

"you'll start to float."

and with that my feet
lifted off the ground

Wonder*Honey*

I used to be terrified of bees
  even though I didn't really take
any time to understand their place
or importance to our world

but then I heard they are dying off
due to pesticides, habitat loss and disease

and suddenly bees became my favorite

scarcity has a way
of turning our deep
fear into fondness
and anxiety into affection

now, I can't imagine
a world without their little bee
butts sticking out of flowers

or the honey they work
so hard to provide me
and my dry toast

or the song they sing
as they buzz past my
ear on the way back home

~ these wiggle bottoms
~ these merchants of sweetness
~ these black/yellow kazoos

are trying to fight
off their fading away

just like me
  just like you
  just like us

I used to run from bees
but now I run to them

  because I don't know how much more time they have left here on earth
and I'll miss them if they are gone   ~ *I'm as surprised as anyone*

 I just can't waste any more time
being afraid of creations that I
don't quite understand

and I'll be more careful
of what and who I will
choose to be scared of

keep bumping and buzzing,
my lovely little amazing bees
and I promise to honor your
 struggle to not vanish
before your job of harvesting
nectar here on earth is done

                            just like me
                            just like you

   just like us

WonderNude One

I caught an angel with long blue hair fingerpainting
the petals onto the flowers in my backyard this morning

*"why do I feel so disconnected
from the Divine?"* I asked

with the paint still dripping off her fingers
she smiled like a baby lighthouse and said

*"because you are trying to
tame a wild and playful God?"*

then she became air
and vanished

after a moment of
absorbing her words
I took off my clothes until I
was as naked as I
imagined God to be

and I spent the rest of the day sunbathing
unafraid under the raw light of creation

and now my tan lines are all gone

Wonder *Text*

a random spam text showed up on my phone this morning:

"hey, do you have time to talk" the message, that
said it was from someone named "Elisabeth" in Yemen stated

"always!" I replied honestly

 I had lots of time

~ more than I'd like to admit

and yes, I know I'm not supposed to reply to these kind of texts

but I've been so lonely lately

like the kind of loneliness that

soaks in your bones and makes

any kind of human contact feel

like a sip of fancy wine that

most people can't quite pronounce

~ it was absolutely delicious

I waited for her response knowing that it could, in fact, be a he or a robot hell, I didn't really

care who it was

a chat sounded

really nice

"Hello, sorry to bother you," Elisabeth responded.

~ oh darling, you aren't ~

you arrived at

just the right time

they continued on:

"Let me introduce myself. I'm Sophia, an HR manager at a recruitment company,"

the person/machine on the other end replied.

~ oh, I thought her name was Elisabeth? now she is Sophia?

how wild

They go on to ask if I needed a part-time job that

"leverages data to optimize app rankings"

how does someone leverage data? is data like

a couch we are trying to get up a narrow staircase?

I decide to change my name too

I want to be a little sexier than "John" and to make me sound important

"Hello, I'm Dante," I offer. "I'm a freelance information distributor and technical manager."

my pulse revved up

                        this started to feel a little dangerous

what's a little roleplay between two complete strangers?

I'm not sure what being a freelance information distributor

or technical manager meant but I was sure that sexy Dante did

I ask Sophia/Elisabeth

how their day was going

"good," they respond

and then fail to ask me

the same question

no matter - I answer it without being asked

I mention that I'm

in a bit of a slump lately

"I feel like I'm stuck in fly paper," I write

silence for five minutes and then "that's too bad,"

sophiabeth texts back

but before I can finish my reply they get back to business

the person sends me a long description of the job opportunity saying that I would help Google/Apple apps flow or increase visibility...and blah blah blah

blah blah boring blah

I don't really care about any of that

I just want to talk about what it's like to wear skin

and feel emotions at the same time

~ so I change the subject and respond with:

"are you having a good day?" I ask

Sophiabeth doesn't reply to that question but

continues texting me about how much money I can make

I ignore her pitch and mash out the following text:

"I'm afraid all of the time - do you know what that's like?"

"no."

oof- brick wall

elisa/sophia/bot continues: "send me your age
and I will forward your name on to my project manager,"

"what's the weather like where you are? it says you are from Yemen, what's that like?"

there's a long pause, and I wonder if she'll answer or
if this conversation will dissolve into digital ether

twenty minutes go by

"yes, Yemen can be very hot,"
she texts back, finally,

for a moment, our script seems to break

"I bet it's always hot in Yemen," I write
back

I want to say more,

but their reply is swift

and automated again

"Please send your age to proceed with job,"

I sigh, the fantasy slipping away,

replaced by the transaction at hand

I decide that the dashing Dante

I'm portraying is young,

but not too young

"26," I type - sensing that our time together

is starting to about to end

that suspicion is

confirmed when she asks:

"and can I get your social security number for my file?"

"I'd rather tell you what I prayed for last
night.

can we put that in my file, instead?" I
inquire

silence

then a final response from elisabotsophie:

"f*** you!"

and then she's gone
like an almost sneeze

but for a brief moment,
in the midst of my solitude,
I allowed myself to believe in a connection,

even if it was with a
ghost in my machine

as I put down my phone,
and say goodbye to Dante
and Sophia Elisabeth

I go back to my loneliness
and I whisper:

"I bet it's always hot in Yemen..."

Wonder*LoveisLove*

I spoke to a person who is convinced their

deceased brother is in hell

simply because of

who they loved

I told them that if hell is real

I don't think it is a destination

I believe hell is a prison

that gets formed in the hearts

of people who judge others

for living a life that they refuse

to try and understand

those who condemn

others to damnation

are the city managers of

hell on Earth

my love,

let us build a heaven

in the space that exists

between my life and yours

let us create an endless garden

paradise where every single

exotic flower is honored

let us form a community of

angels who don't try to

polish each other's halos

we only have

so many heartbeats

left inside of us

to waste a single one

on deciding who gets

to grow like a sunflower

under the light of the hereafter

who knows what happens

to us once our bodies release

our souls like birthday party balloons?

~ why spend an ounce of energy

on deciding who gets to go to heaven

when we can spend our lives

building it here on Earth

with the bricks of how we

treat each other?

until I hear the harps

and see the golden gates

I'm going to consider this

world the Promised Land

**and I promise to be
as kind**

**as I can be with
your heart**

**while we are here
together**

Wonder *Voice*

I no longer pray to
hear God's voice

~ *I pray to hear mine* ~

Because when I hear
my own voice
□
it means that despite
all of my wounds

~ I'm still here:

seeking
asking
fighting
loving

maybe for me,

God is a canyon wall
that I get to echo
my shaking voice off of

and maybe that is

all I need right now

Wonder*Feelings*

an open poem to a world-weary empath,

you can't leave Earth yet

~ because I just flipped ahead about a hundred pages in your story and I read that someday you will be the reason someone else doesn't give up on their life

I'm sorry to spoil the end of your epic tale

~ but someday you will be the one who ignites the blaze in another person's heart that won't ever be put out again

don't complicate the plot of your story

~ you are here to be a lamplighter who hands out little bits of your flame to ensure the rest of the world doesn't exist in darkness

I know you have been scorched so many times

~ to love the world is to sometimes be burned at the stake by others who mistake your gift of compassion as a personal weakness

I know it's not easy to be a bringer of light to those who have become addicted to shadows

~ but we need you to be a gardener of effervescent seeds that you will perhaps never see grow into burning rose bushes that can be seen from space

Oh, my love, don't give into the calling despair

~ set your life on fire with kindness and watch how many other people come out of their caves to sit by your campfire heart to share their own stories of survival

Oh my love, you are my favorite element

WonderSong

once there was a forest that
was the home to a pretty little robin

one day the little robin asked God:

> *"What song*
> *would You like*
> *me to sing for you?"*

God responded to her as a falling rose petal.

> *"Oh, my dear*
> *little Robin, I love you*
> *but don't sing Me a song."*

The robin was confused.

> *"But I have so many songs*
> *I could serenade You with.*
> *I have a lovely ballad about the*
> *sunrise that will make even You cry."*

> *"That's okay, my little one.*
> *I don't want you to sing Me a song."*
> *God said quietly to her through*
> *the swarming spring breeze.*

"God must not be able to hear me correctly."
the little robin thought.

She flew up to the
top of the highest tree
in the park and asked

"God, can I offer You a hymn
on how much I love my wings?
It is such a beautiful song."

God spoke to the little robin
through a single beam of sunlight.

"No, little robin, I
don't want you to
sing me a song.
In fact, I don't want
you to sing a song
ever again."

The little heart inside
of the little robin broke.

She had been practicing her
whole life to become a beautiful
singer.

The little robin felt so lost.

"If I am not to sing
what is my purpose?

God came down to the little robin
in the form of a single drop of rain
that landed on her tiny beak and said:

"I don't want you to just sing
a song - I want you to become a song."

Suddenly the little
robin felt a warmth
inside her that she

had never felt before.

It was peace.
It was peace.
It was purpose
It was peace.
it was a fire

the little robin began to glow
and then just like that she split into four
equal pieces

the first piece was a falling rose petal
the second piece was a gentle breeze
the third piece was a radiating sunbeam
and the last piece was a single drop of rain

and it was all music

and that was the day when
the little robin became the most
beautiful song any
animal in the forest
had ever heard

Wonder*Saint*

I fell through a hole in
a church pew yesterday

and landed right
in the thick amber
field of a piece of
stained glass

I asked a red saint
who was stargazing

"why must I suffer?"

without looking
at me
he said

"to know God."

I didn't like
that answer

so

I crawled through
a mist of royal triangles
and swam across a sea of ovals
and scaled a pointed cusp

until I found a glowing sinner
and I asked her the
same question

"why must I suffer?"

she placed her
green hand on my
purple cheek
and sung

*"because a broken heart
is easier to share."*

suddenly
my hands became
turquoise doves

and my lips became
yellow vines

and my feet became
fat red rubies

and I became radiant
painted glass of the divine

and I became
reflected light

and everything
I touched glowed

**and now my broken
illuminated heart
colors the walls**

of every room I walk into

Wonder*Broken*

I was born with a hole in my heart
that kept my parents from having
a decent night of sleep for the
first year of my life

they would each take turns
sitting next to my crib
every evening watching me
sleep to ensure that my
heart would remember
to keep beating

my dad would steady one
hand softly on my chest
and the other on one of his
cheap World War II
spy novel he'd likely be reading
and waiting for my mom to relieve
him for her shift at around 3 a.m.

every time I sneezed they thought
my body would turn into a firecracker

each time I cried they waited for
death to slip in under the door to
collect their little boy

they were waiting for
the other shoe
to drop

I was real-life
version of Russian roulette

it was only a matter
of time before the hole
in my heart would break
theirs into pieces

my parents weren't
walking on eggshells

they were line dancing on them

after I survived the first
year my parents started
to relax a bit around their
son with a holey heart

maybe I wasn't just an undetonated bomb of grief waiting to detonate

~ maybe my story wouldn't
just be all prologue

~ maybe I would make it

still, my incomplete heart
was never far from their full attention

I remember on my first day of elementary school
when my mom showed up at lunch to
tell my teacher that I had to sit on the bench at recess

because of you know...my heart hole

so I sat and watched everybody
chase each other

Isabella came over
to ask me to join

in the great
run with them

I can't remember her
last name but I remember
her long jet black hair

"I can't," I said

"Why?" Isabella asked

"I have a hole in my heart," I said

"Oh, sorry."

That was the response I get whenever
I tell people that I'm unwell.

"Oh, sorry."

What else is somebody
supposed to say
when I turn our small talk
into a confessional?

"Hello John."

"I'm broken."

"Oh, sorry."

The older I got the less
my parents began to outwardly
fret about the gap in my ticker

they relaxed
~ but not really

they kept waiting
for the heartbreak to
show up

they kept waiting for
the other shoe to drop

my heart with a hole in it
would only get brought
up when I let them down

which turned out to be a lot

it became a point
of leverage for them

flashforward to
the day when

I was 22 when they showed up unannounced
at the door of my college apartment speaking in tandem

"We saw your midterms."

"Uh huh."

"Why did you drop
out of that class?"

"Because it was stupid
~ and the professor didn't like me
~ and it was too hard
~ and I don't understand why I need to take it
~ and I just needed a break from studying
~ and I will take it later and it's not a big deal."

and - and - and

*"You are failing
half of your classes,"they said*

*"I like to look at it
like I'm passing half
of them,"I snarked*

"Don't be smart with us."

"Right."

*"Are you going to
be able to graduate
from college next semester?"*

"Probably not."

*"Do you know how
much we took care
of you when you
were a baby?"*

"Yes, of course."

*"Do you know
how many nights
we prayed for your
heart to not stop?"*

"Yes, of course."

*"Do you know how much
stress you have caused us?"*

"Yes, of-"

"Do you know that
your brother is getting
his masters next week
and you can't be even bothered
to finish your undergraduate classes."

"I know..."

"You are really letting
us down. "

"I know - but -"

"Why are you doing this to us ?"

"I think there is something
wrong with me. That's why."

long pause

"Oh, sorry."

                    then the three of us
                    said the worst thing
                    we could have
                    in that moment
                    in the doorway of my
                    college apartment:

~ nothing

                    we stood there is
                    silence

                I had finally broken their
                heart

their fretting and worrying
became fully realized

~ it took a while but shoe did eventually meet floor

what I couldn't explain to
them at the time was
that I had a second
hole in me forming
that scared me a lot more
than my first one

this time the hole
was in my brain

the hole in my mind
was less of a murmur
and more like a monster

it was a hole
that wanted to
consume me whole

it was a hole
that had several
rows of crooked teeth
that left bite marks
on my stomach
whenever I tried to
get out of bed

I never told either of them
about it because they had
already worried their lives
away on me

I just closed the door and
they went back home and
I went back inside to
lay down in a dry
bathtub listening to
the holes in
my head and heart
write love letters
to each other

****

a full two years later
I was in Taize, France
on a pilgrimage

I traveled there with
a church group
but in reality I was
there on my own

I had come around the
world to talk to
God who had
apparently started
wearing camouflage

I had recently started
to experience a new
hole forming inside of me

this time it was in
an unseeable place
inside of me

my soul

this hole hurt
the most

all the magic
and miracle
and joy of living
and faith
that I used to feel
were leaking out of me
and into the sky above

I had come around the
world to tell God to patch
me up

but I was met with the exact
same absence I had back
home

God never showed up
with a first aid kit

My dad had died
a month before
my journey

the experiences
I had surrounding
his death were still
laying heavy on me

I had so many
regrets that they
had to take turns
tying themselves
to my back

~ so many unspoken words

which truth be told
was the genesis of
my trip to Taize

I had come around the
world to tell God to tell
him I'm sorry I wasn't
a better son

but God wasn't accepting
my phone calls

I could feel the hole
in my heart widening
and the one in my head
and the one in my soul
I was nothing but holes now

they would soon merge
and I would be gone

sitting there among
truly holy people
With my broken heart

I was the holeyest of them all

there were people
from all walks of
life and faiths
sitting in the beautiful
candle lit temple

it looked the part
of where mystical

experiences take place
on a routine basis

during the day we
would labor around
the camp site

hundred of us would be
cooking
cleaning rooms
building structures
scrubbing bathrooms

and then four times a day
the bell would ring to call
is to temple where
we would sit there
long periods of either
silence or simple song

the songs were
usually just a line
or two of lyrics
that would be repeated
over and over
for 10-20 minutes

I sang the words
hoping I could
at the very least
brainwash myself
into believing things
would be okay

I didn't need God
to be real

I just needed to go
back believing that
God was real

I decided there was
a difference between
the two

I spent every session
for five days
singing for my life

hoping that the
words would make
a garden inside of me

but I had too
many holes for
rosebushes to
grow

on my last night there
something happened

I remember the song
we were singing when
the old man next
grabbed my hand
and held it tightly in his

"Bless the Lord, my soul
And bless God's holy name
Bless the Lord, my soul
Who leads me into life"

He was crying;
actually sobbing is a

better description
of what he was doing

it wasn't sorrowful weeping
he was crying with a wide smile
revealing his toothless mouth

I could feel the calluses
in his palm rub
against my smooth skin

I felt ashamed

the contrast between
the condition of our
hands felt like an indictment
of my life

it didn't seem to phase the old man
one bit as his hand kept squeezing mine
in rhythm to the song

"Bless the Lord (squeeze), my soul (hand squeeze)
And Bless God's (squeeze) holy name (hand squeeze)
Bless the Lord (squeeze), my soul (hand squeeze)
Who (hand squeeze) leads me (hand squeeze) me back into (long hand squeeze) life.

The song went on for
about ten minutes

I would like to say that
I squeezed his hand back

but I didn't

I was too uncomfortable
and distracted

his hands were very dirty
his robes were covered in mud
his body didn't smell very good

the old man kept crying
- and kept squeezing my hand

and I just
wanted it to end

eventually it did

we all got up to leave
the old man was still
holding my hand
and gave it one
last super squeeze

I gave him the fakest
smile I could produce

it was Oscar worthy

I then offered him a bow
like he was some sort
of enlightened master

he shook his head
and poked me in
the chest

hard

~ ow

and despite my

trying to back out
of it the man lurched
forward and hugged me

the only way to describe
the way this man held me
was to say it felt like I was
being swaddled by a hundred
million fireflies

there was an energy
in his unwashed arms

the base of my spine
was like a rocket that
wanted to take off

my skin tingled
like every particle
inside of me was
getting a kiss from
heaven

I know that sounds
ridiculous

when we stopped
hugging I suddenly became
concerned that I was going to
pass out

I was going to be
one of those people
who hit the ground
after a faith healer
slaps them in a
white suit slaps them

upside the face with
some southern spirit

my body was shaking

the man poked my chest again
harder (ow) and said something to
me in a language I could not
understand

a lady about half his age
who had been sitting on the other
side of him the entire time
waved at me

she said in jumbled english:

*"Do you want to know
what he said?"*

"Yes, of course."

*"He said let all of the incomplete things in you
become an instrument.
Tie all your broken pieces together and become a wind chime."*

I smiled
this time it was real.

With that the lady took the
old man by the hand and
they disappeared in the crowd.

My spine spoke up again:

*"Be an ocarina. An instrument whose many holes
in turn the wind into music."*

"Be a wind chime. Bless the world with
the gently clanging sound of grace passing through you."

"You are not a decoration. You are a wounded apparatus of melody and song.
Your gaps will hum with spirit."

I was ready to levitate straight up through the roof of the chapel. I was a kite
begging to kiss a star field.

My spine went back to sleep
- but the fire remained.

I asked the wind to turn the holes in me into music. I begged grace to turn me
into sound.

I sat back down to
sing on my own

and that's when the visions came

Bless the Lord (I could see my parents sitting by my crib) my soul (I could feel my
dads hand on my newborn chest)

And Bless Gods holy name (I could rushing over to me whenever I cried)

Bless the Lord (I could see my mom wring her hands on my first day of school)who
leads us back to life (I could see my parents wiping the tears from their face as I
shut my college apartment door on them)

forgiveness washed over me

my parents loved me

they did their absolute
best to protect me

they didn't know what to
do with the holes forming in me

that's okay -
because neither did I

I was never a very good son
to either of my parents

I asked God to tell my dad

that I was sorry
oh (so) sorry
oh (so) sorry
oh (so) sorry

I was assured that
my dad would get the message

it was in that moment
as I sat in a near empty
temple on the other side
of the world
that the gaping holes
in my heart
and my mind
and in my soul

all became an ocarina
and my wounds became wind chimes

and for one night I became the most beautiful song that I've ever heard
and from that moment on the conversation goes like this:

"Hello John."

"I'm broken."

"Oh, sorry."

"I'm not."

Wonder*Politics*

my politics
are the least
interesting thing
about me

I'll be disappointed if

the angel who
scoops me off
of my quiet
deathbed

asks me who I voted for

instead, I hope
my exit interview
consists of only
one question

"Did you heal more than you hurt?"

~ because those are exactly my politics

Wonder*Request*

hope doesn't ever ask
very for much from us

except

for us to keep
the door open

WonderHope

I accidentally became friends with my despair
after spending so much time together recently.

Last night, while the two of us were lying
together in the dark on my bathroom floor - despair told me a secret:

"My name used to be Hope," my despair revealed.

"When did you change your name?" I asked.

"The moment I became homeless," my despair wept.

~ oh my love,
I think I finally figured it out.

**despair is just hope
that lost its home.**

Wonder*Islands*

I just read that researchers claimed to have
 discovered that there are 7000 more
islands in Japan than we
previously had thought that there were

> *~ I immediately thought of you*

and how you keep finding new
 lands in your ancient heart to go explore

My love, you are my favorite
unfolding and

   ~unsolvable mystery

Wonder*Priests*

put children in charge of
all our churches
and watch

how playful God becomes

Wonder*Pain*

"Mr. Roedel, how would you rate your pain on a scale of 1-10?" the nurse asked me yesterday as I flopped and floundered on the E.R. exam table I was sitting on.

"17,819!" I yelped as the kidney stone inside of me performed a triple somersault on the unforgiving mat that is my urinary tract.

The nurse looked up from her electronic tablet she was mashing out notes on to give me a quick glance of silent disapproval. She turned her finger into a ruler and pointed at the chart on the wall that showed a slew of faces in various states of discomfort.

"Let's stick to the 0-10 scale, please," she said in a tone that reminded me of how my elementary school teachers used to speak to me.

"Please give me a serious answer," the nurse said after I remained silent. It was the second time in a row she used "please" while speaking to me. This was not a good sign.

I put on my glasses and looked at the pain chart more closely. I wanted to be a compliant patient, so I decided to take a bit more time to reflect on my pain value.

0-1: No Pain. The face was smiling like it had just drunk a pina colada poolside. The free and easy smile on this face was a little smug for my taste. This face seemed to suffer from a bit of toxic positivity.

2-3: Mild pain. The face was very similar to the first "no pain face"—except the smile was a bit crooked. Everything was going pretty well for this face, except for a little annoying pang of human discomfort that it couldn't seem to shake. I could immediately identify with this face. This is my baseline state of living. No matter how great things can go for me—there is always one fly in the ointment. They should just call this "Mild Pain" face the "Mid-Life" face.

4-5: Moderate Pain. Now this face was starting to go through it. This isn't an inconvenient pain that someone could excuse away. The expression on this little character is an example of when the mask we try to hide under starts to melt away. This reminded me of the face I make every time I eat a piece of black licorice.

6-7: Severe Pain. This face can't even hide it anymore. The pain is starting to overtake them. What started as a rainstorm has turned into a flood. There is no room for being polite when it comes to this type of pain.

8-9: Intense Pain. I am not sure what the difference would be between "Severe Pain" and "Intense Pain" except to say that this face looks like it is mired in hopelessness. I suppose that is the worst type of suffering. The kind that doesn't feel like it will ever end. This is the type of pain where bladder control functions become "optional."

10: The Worst Pain Ever. This must be the rock bottom of all suffering. I think I felt this kind of pain that leads our brains to shut down and send us into shock because it can't keep up with the production of agony.

I kept studying the pain chart. It felt like a test. I didn't want to get this answer wrong. If I gave too low of a number, they may not believe me that the kidney stone inside of me was the antichrist. I was worried that if I gave too high of a number (which I already had done) it would make her think I was auditioning for a part in a melodrama.

I had a brief breeze of courage that washed over me and encouraged me to try and impress this nurse with my pain tolerance.

"Um..."

"Just pick a number," my nurse said while starting to grip her e-tablet like a stress plush.

"My pain level keeps changing," I answered honestly.

"What is it right now?"

"I would say that my pain is at a 5.5 with a couple of hints of 6.7," I offered.

"So should we average it out at 6?" she asked.

"6.2," I replied. We were suddenly negotiating.

"Fine, 6.2," she sighed as she considered changing her vocation.

After another prolonged, awkward exchange of the two of us talking about any possible allergies that I might have, she left the room to likely inform the doctor I was about to see how terrible of a patient I was.

I was alone in the room with my growling kidney stone and the stupid pain chart that I was now obsessed with.

I started to chart each wave of pain as it arrived on the tender shores of my central nervous system. I compared my face to the corresponding cartoon face on the chart.

"6....5....7...7....5...ugh 7.5," I whispered under my jagged breath. I felt terrible. Like a badger was performing an improvised surgery on my insides.

A different nurse came back a few moments later to let me know that the doctor would be in soon. This nurse wore a much more compassionate expression in her eyes than my previous one.

"I would like to change my pain number," I requested as I rocked back and forth. "I think I was trying to be brave earlier."

"Sure, honey, what is it now?"

"7.5," I lamented while trying to hold back my tears.

"Thank you for being honest," she smiled. "Locking your pain inside of you will make your body a prison."

Her words hit me like the softest of velvet hammers.

The nurse updated my chart and walked out of the room. I sat under the pain chart and wrote the following quick poem with my trembling little hands:

Sometimes poems come to me at the strangest times.

A day and one passed-kidney stone later, I am still reflecting on the idea of how we often hide our pain from each other.

"How are you doing?" people often ask us.

"Fine," we often lie.

We don't want to burden others with our suffering, so we bury it deep inside the graveyard of our hearts.

Maybe we should be asking each other what our pain number is. Because we are all usually dealing with some sort of suffering—and maybe it's not actually anything we can put words to. But we can give it a number.

"What's your pain level today?" people could ask us.

"5," we might say in reply, trying to hold up our smiles like those little cartoon faces.

Then we hug. Because we all know what a "5" feels like.

Oh, my love,

what is your pain number today?

Wonder*River*

I had been carrying hope
in my pocket like it was
polished gemstone for years

whenever trouble came
I'd squeeze hope tightly
in my shaking hand

and I could feel
it bump against my
palm like a newborn
heartbeat

that's how
I knew that
I was safe

recently though,
I somehow lost my hope

   I have no idea if I put it down
somewhere or if it slipped out
while I was fumbling for my keys

without being able
to hold onto hope

I soon became lost myself

after a while of wandering
in the wild on my own

I bumped into hope
  ~ who looked so different

hope was no longer a
little gemstone that could
Fit in my pants pocket

hope was a now a wide stream
cutting through the woods

                    "I thought I lost you!" I admonished

the river grabbed a couple of
rainbow trout and used them
to smile at me

              "lost me?" The water babbled. "That's impossible!"

        "Well, one minute I was holding onto you and the next you were gone."

              "I needed to change forms," Hope replied.

                    "Why?" I asked.

"Because you've been carrying me for so long that I decided we should try something different."

                    "What's that?"

          "I thought I would take a turn carrying you for a bit."

the river rose
up around me

and pulled me gently onto
my back

I was floating

I didn't realize how exhausted I was
until the river held me

and hope carried me
and hope carried me
and hope carried me

~now whenever trouble comes

I just spread my arms open
and let hope wrap me up in
her slow water

and I can still feel it
pulse against me like a
newborn heartbeat

that's how
I know that
I'm safe

I don't know where
we are going

hope and I
still appear to
be lost

but at least we
are together

maybe we will stay lost out
here for a while longer

funny enough, I'm in no rush

to get to our destination

because it has been so long
since I've felt held by anything

and I think I could really

get used

to it

Wonder*Magic*

I didn't believe in magic
until I was forgiven by someone

I didn't believe that incantations worked
until I forgave another person

-now my sorcery is mercy

-now my wizardry is pardoning

-now I am the spellcaster of clemency

and now for my next trick

**I will make both
of our regrets
disappear**

Wonder*Math*

I used to think that
spirituality was about
finding answers

but I've surprisingly found

so much comfort in
the unanswerable
questions of this life

faith is an endless
curvy dirt country road

*~ with countless roadside
oddities for me to marvel at ~*

*~ and moments of danger
where the wolves are
chewing on my heels~*

*~and trees that grow up
out of the wasteland
just for me to nap under~*

*~and bookend sunrises and
sunsets that serve
as a wink from the nod
from the divine that
encourages me to
keep exploring the
mystery of this whole
sprawling adventure ~*

life isn't a riddle

to be deciphered

we don't solve for X here

we are just asked to keep searching
   because the more we do
the more we get to see

we can't find God by
turning the comfort of
our couch into a chapel

                 with all so respect to U2,

                 ~we must climb highest mountains
                 ~we must run through the fields
                 ~we must scale these city walls

                 and even if we do all of that

                 we are likely to never find
                 exactly what it is we are searching for

~ that notion used to break my heart ~

not anymore

now I'm set free by the everlasting mystery
of our existence here in Earth

when I was in grade school
I used to love that math books
had all of the answers to the problems
located in the back of the book

I became tethered to exact knowledge

~not anymore

now I'm treating life like
an unsolvable equation

  ~ like a nonsensical run-on word problem:

> *"if John has a heart*
> *that broke into 245 pieces*
> *and each of those pieces contained*
> *5,000 memories of times when*
> *the sun peeked through the trees*
> *at just the right angle to make it feel*
> *like an angels was kissing his cheek*
> *then how many of John's tears can*
> *be used to grow a garden?"*

the thing is, I've been
searching so hard for
the face of creation since
the moment I was born

that my skin has become
a rippling river that carries me
around each new bend and
into a new valley or surprises
and never the ocean from where
I first came from

    oh, I still haven't found what I'm looking for
    and it's likely that I never will while I'm alive

        and that is a prospect that is
          so exciting to me
        that I can't hardly breathe

Wonder*Genesis*

Long before there were
  any stars

When the great empty void
  was packed full of a hundred-thousand
other even emptier voids

There was a soft whisper in the dark

  ~ and maybe this whisper was more like a song
  ~ and maybe this song was more like a poem
  ~ and maybe this poem was more like a prayer

And this soft whisper
~that was a song
~that was a poem
~that was a prayer

kept uttering your name and saying

"I can't wait for the
day you come to find me"

yes, even before
the first crack of
Genesis lightning
spread its dandelion
seed across the cosmos

you were the first thing
on the mind of a waking God

oh, my love,

please hold on
you matter more than matter itself

please hold on
you have more time than time itself

please hold on
you have existed before existence

please hold on

Wonder*Elements*

there are three rivers

the one river below us
is made up of water and earth

the one river above us
Is made up of wind and fire

and the one river inside us
is made up of each of the four elements

creation flows below us
creation flows above us
creation flows within us

it's my favorite kind
of tangled knot

where each string
is made up of the
most everlasting
of cosmic fabrics

my love,

the elements have turned
our hearts into a stretching
park bench where are all welcome
to come and sit together for a spell

~ and if we rest so very quietly there

we can hear the soundtrack
to our time here on this planet
call out to us

the flowing water of our singular existence
the groaning earth of our sacred story
the roaring wind of our rushing empathy
the crackling fire of our soul's purpose

there are three rivers

one below us
one above us
one within us

and they are all carrying us back to
the same ocean womb where we
we were formed out of holy mud
long long ago

so, my love, let's put down our paddles for a bit and just enjoy the current

there is no race to win
there is no trophy to collect
there is no status to be earned

there is only the flow
of the river below, above
and inside of us

~ someday I'll meet you at the sea

Wonder*Naked* Two

someone just told me
to "pull myself together"

and I immediately started laughing
because I'm not that person anymore

there is nothing
to put back

>   those old pieces are
>   are all lost

>   and I have no interest
>   in finding them ever again

>   do snakes try and slip back
>   into their freshly shed skin?

~ my strings have been cut
~ the mask has slipped off
~ my disguise is on the bedroom floor

>   I'm walking around
>   in only my cozy socks

>   this is my
>   only magic trick:

>   to joyfully deconstruct
>   right in front of you

>   and now leaning into a

version of myself
that I was made to
be so long ago

~ self-loved
unafraid
~ singing

and a whirling witness to
the miracle of creation

as I wear nothing but
my birthday suit

finally unclothed
finally unleashed
finally unfolded
finally unashamed

finally understood

finally
finally
finally

~ naked

and ready to skinny-dip
under a blazing moon

Wonder*Lost*

God keeps throwing all of
my maps into the campfire

Wonder*Flood*

when I was a child I was told that grace came
slowly to those of us who earned it quickly

it was explained to me that grace was a transactional relationship
between a divine producer and a good boy consumer

if the good boy paid his debts on time then grace would be delivered
to him in small bits that he would then be called on to pass on to others that
he had deemed fit to receive it

it was a form of trickledown salvation

it was a pyramid scheme
of blessings

> *"take a little glory*
> *John, and pass it on,*
> *not too much*
> *though, we're*
> *rationing for*
> *winter"*

instead, I've come to find that actual grace comes with no
strings or fine print attached

> *grace isn't a contract*
> *grace is an endless well*

it's more transformative
than it is transactional

grace isn't a knot
grace is the flow

when I was young, grace was described
to me as a thin creek that I needed to bring my
own pan and sifter to if I wanted to find a couple
specks of gold hidden by God laying in the
bed of uniform rocks

that I needed to be careful in looking
for too much of it or I'd fall into
the river and drown

I was instructed that
grace was reserved for
the master gold hunter
                    and not the amateur hobbyist

what I have learned however,

is that grace is
the breaking dam of
rushing treasure

and it's available to all

                regardless of our status

                    regardless of our station

grace was never the rare gold
hidden away for only the few

grace has always been the abundant water
and there is enough to go around for all of us

grace is pouring out from

the mouth of the universe
without end

grace is all rush

                    and the valley is filling up
                    and the water is transforming us
                    and I'm not afraid of drowning anymore

grace is the blessed water
and it's rising to meet us and
it's the flood of timeless
mercy and sacred love and
it's ready to start
sweeping us away

                    and I can't hardly wait
                    and the water is all around us
                    and I'm being lifted up off the ground
                    and it's carrying me away
                    and I'm ready to go

to wherever grace will take me

Wonder*Survival*

Today, I feel terribly exhausted with a
bit of melancholy chaser.

I also feel very anxious with a
little hint of jealousy mixed in
for good measure.

Today, I am crippled with fear
and a whiff of anger that
keeps lingering around me like a
junior high school dance cologne.

I feel both mortally wounded
with new injuries as well as
ravaged with aching old scars.

Today, I'm unwell.
Today, I'm a big mess.
Today, I'm a little devastated.

Today, I'm overwhelmed with this world.
Today, I'm underwhelmed with myself.

Today, I'm am tempted to give up.
Today, I'm being seduced by despair.

- but I'm
still here.

And so are you.

Despite everything we've endured - we are still holding on.

We are still here.

I'm calling the Vatican.
   because our survival is a miracle.

My love,
you are a marvel.

Your courage to keep going is a phenomenon.

Your next breath is a wonder flower.

Your next heartbeat is a revelation.

I'm so proud of you.

Of us.

After everything that tried to consume us

- We are still here.

We are miracles.

WonderGeese

I've spent all morning watching a flock of geese
bathe in a lake her in North Carolina
- and it all feels like a prayer.

Some geese stand
with one leg in the water,

some geese lay out on the shore,
some geese float into the wash.

I'm not an avian scientist, bird psychologist, or goose theologian - so I can't quite
know - but it would appear as if none of the geese are stuck in their past mistakes.

Nor do any of them seem overly consumed with worry about their future.

These geese are just bathing in cool water under a raging fireball that rests above
them in the bluest of blankets. They aren't fighting over whose water it is. They
aren't trying to define what the sun and the sky are for each other. They aren't
trying to solve every mystery.

From what I can see, there are no hard rules for being a goose this morning -
except this:

be here now and let me be here now.

Now the Geese are waddling away together to find shade. Some geese are picking
at the grass. Others are staring up into the sky. I imagine it all has to be such a
wonder for them. I hope it is. I bet it is.

The way they crane their necks all around them to see everything indicates to me
that geese are obsessed with wonder. I'm so jealous.

Now the flock has moved beyond my sightline and into the woods. I'm really sad they are gone. It was like watching a sunset. It was like listening to a piece of music. It was the last sip of coffee in the morning.

It was like hearing back from God for the first time in such a long time.

I've been calling out. Looking. Seeking. For so long. I've been looking for one single breadcrumb to lead me to somewhere I can feel seen by Creation.

And now I do. At least I did for a melting ice cube moment where the First Breath told me to quit time traveling and to

Be here now.

That particular now was so lovely. I simply need to find more of them to pay attention to. I wonder where they are. I wonder if they are all around me. I wonder.

Oh, how I love to wonder. Frankly, I'm suddenly obsessed with it.

Maybe that makes me part goose?

Wonder*Lungs*

for years we have been told
that home is where the heart is
~ but I don't think that's true

home is where our lungs are

my love, whenever I get lost in
the wilds of the world and I can't find my way

I inhale so slowly
        ~ so deeply

and suddenly
I'm right back at home

because I was born out
of the holy breath of the Divine

as were you,
my love
as were you

the breath of Mystery
is our eternal home

the place we
existed

long before we
we ever existed

an angel once told me that

we were formed so carefully
while we rested in the gusting womb
of the Great Love's sacred gale

our home is the place
where Source gently
exhaled us into existence

we were created out
the of holiest of thin air to
become dandelion seeds moving
in the currents of adventure

carrying us from one
horizon the the next

> *~ and whenever the*
> *storms of this world*
> *become too much of*
> *us to endure*

> *~ whenever the woods become*
> *so dark that we can no longer*
> *see the sky*

> *~ whenever we get*
> *so lost in the*
> *wilderness that the*
> *compass we are holding*
> *turns into sand between*
> *our fingers*

> *~ whenever we find*
> *ourselves so homesick*
> *that we can't remember*
> *what it feels like to be safe*

we can just breathe a
big fat breath and
hold it in our chest
for a couple moments

and suddenly
my love,
~ so very suddenly

we return home

we go right
back to where
we first started

to he gusting cottage of the Great Love

because the same air that passes through our trembling lips
and into our lungs is the exact same air that Creation
breathed on us when we sparked out of the great void

so, my love,

when you lose
your way out
here in the swirl

and your so desperate
to return home

~ to the familiar place
where you felt so safe

~ to the warm dwelling where
you knew everything about
yourself

~ to the cradle where
nothing could ever harm you

you don't have to
click your heels

or buy a plane ticket
or make a wish

you just have to
breathe with purpose
and treat the air
inside of you as
if it were a prayer

and when you exhale
that held breath

oh my love,
whenever you exhale

you'll come right back home

Wonder*Peace* One

we are watching warfare play out on tik tok
we are live-tweeting during the fall of *Rome*

we are building our echo chambers on YouTube
we are bloodletting through a camera of a *drone*

I have never believed that the devil exists
but I no longer have the luxury of being *aloof*;

as our indifference toward this wheel of hate
for me, has become a convincing article of *proof*

~ evil isn't always an open, slobbering and screaming mouth
~ evil doesn't always show up at our door looking like a hungry *bear*

~ evil will often wear an ornate altar robe to hide their sharp sword
~ evil can be a sermon of vengeance that's disguised as a *prayer*

~ war is usually the wailing love child of two ancient wars
~ that had a one-night stand under a dripping blood *moon*

~ revenge is a planet-killing comet that only creates new comets
~ an eye for an eye will leave us all completely blind *soon*

I don't have any answer to this riddle of violence
I don't know how to avert this slow-motion *doomsday*

I hope we will start to dig gardens instead of trenches
I am begging that soon we will embrace a gentler *way*

I can't believe that searching for peace is a fool's errand
I am okay being a cliche of a man wearing Peace Dove *tights*

I will keep begging to Creation to thaw this winter of our hate
and to remind us that we forged to become children of lights

Wonder*Peace* Two

I can't make the
world be peaceful

I can't stall tanks
from roaring down roads

I can't prevent children
from having to hide in bunkers

I can't convince the news to
stop turning war into a video game

I can't silence the sound of bombs
tearing neighborhoods apart

I can't turn a guided missile
into a bouquet of flowers

I can't make a warmonger
have an ounce of empathy

I can't convince diplomats
to quit playing truth or dare

I can't deflect a sniper's bullet
from turning a wife into a widow

I can't stave off a schoolyard being
reduced to ash and rubble

I can't do any of that

the only thing I can do
is love the next person I encounter
without any conditions or strings

to love my neighbor
so fearlessly that
it starts a ripple
that stretches from
one horizon to the next

I can't force peace
on the world

*but I can become a force
of peace in the world*

because

sometimes all it takes
is a single lit candle
in the darkness

to start a movement

oh, Spirit,

let me be a candle
of comfort in this world

let me burn with peace

Wonder*Counts*

(how self help works in these days)

screaming into
our pillows until we
lose our voices

~ counts as prayer

going outside every evening to
watch a sunset fight against
the pull of the inevitable horizon

~ counts as watching the news

spending an extra ten minutes
in the shower in the morning,
to keep them from seeing us cry

~ counts as leisure time

saying "thank you" and "I love you"
to the people we need to say those
things to while they're still alive

~ counts as replying to an email

pouring out the contents of
our hearts to a gravestone
once or twice a year

~ counts as decluttering

spending time with a friend
who doesn't take it personally
that we are changing

~ counts as getting a massage

dripping hot wax from a dying candle
on the top of our hands in order to stop the
feeling of our skin crawling off our body

~ counts as self care

gracefully avoiding all of the triggers
and traps that despair
lays out in our path every day

~ counts as dancing

looking for angels
who are living
among us

~ counts as birdwatching

digging our fingers into our arms
whenever we receive a bill we know we
won't be able pay on time

~ counts as balancing our checkbooks

removing
judgemental people
in our life

~ counts as starting a new diet

tracing heart shapes on the

middle of our forehead
while laying in bed at night

~ *counts as supporting the arts*

trying to catch our jagged breath
to keep ourselves from having
a massive panic attack before work

~ *counts as jogging*

sitting under a tree in the park
and listening to music
on a September morning

~ *counts as going to church*

learning to unconditionally love
ourselves despite all of the scars
that we carry around with us

~ *counts as being born again*

letting children see
the tears fall from our
eyes without any shame

~ *counts as parenting*

swallowing all of the unkind words
we have for people who absolutely
drive us crazy

~ *counts as taking vitamins*

holding a sleeping
newborn baby

in our hands

~ counts as drinking water

turning off our
cellphones and putting
them in a drawer

~ counts as going camping

writing out the names of
everyone who counts on
us to not surrender to despair

~ counts as updating our resumes

spending time exploring
all of the uncharted places
in our hearts

~ counts as traveling to a foreign country

closing our eyes for a fat second
to avoid seeing the look on someone's face
when we admit to feeling feeling unwell

~ counts as taking a nap

holding a picture of someone
you lost contact with and whispering
"I'm so sorry" over and over

~ counts as closure

looking at our naked form
in the mirror for two minutes
without loathing what we see

~ counts as being romantic

chewing on our fingernails
until they look like a
disappearing shoreline

~ counts as getting a manicure

scribbling down every single
wish we have for ourselves
on a coffeehouse napkin

~ counts as investing in a 401k

spending time walking
among songbirds before
the first light of day

~ counts as social networking

getting back in our feet
after the world had knocked
us down for the 4000th time

~ counts as maintaining a routine

everything we do in 2022
to keep ourselves from giving up

counts

this modern world is an churning ocean
of constant chaos and raging water

my love, if we want to make it to the next horizon
we'll have to build our life rafts out of whatever

materials we can find

~ it all counts

be kind to yourself
as you hold it all together

to keep your heart from sinking
amid the tempest is a sacred act of survival

keep going

no matter how weird it looks;
every paddle you take
toward shore counts

keep going

don't worry about how awkward
your survival looks to other people

keep going

~ it all counts
everything you are doing to stay with us

counts

persist, my love
because
you are meant to exist

keep going
I love you
keep going

Wonder*Feast*

My soul slipped out of my body so it could finally sit down and speak to me face to face.

I was surprised how thin my soul appeared now that I could actually look at it with my eyes. It was so much skinnier than I thought it would be.

"Why aren't you feeding me?" my soul asked.

I could tell it was struggling to maintain its illuminated outline. My soul flickered in and out like a fading truck stop bathroom light.

"I am," I replied. "Don't you remember last week when I let us watch that little self-guided meditation on YouTube that was about how to maintain a positive attitude or something?"

To be honest, I couldn't quite remember what it was that I had watched - because I had fallen asleep about 45 seconds into the video.

My soul sighed.

"That's not enough for me to keep my light blazing. What you have been giving me are crumbs. What I need is a banquet of beauty and wonder to feast on. I require a sprawling clambake of miracles and revelation to maintain my connection to Creation. I am starving for a fat spread of delicious marvel and decadent awe," my Soul went on to say.

"Wow, I didn't know you were such a diva," I snapped.

"I'm not a diva. I'm malnourished," it said to me while beginning to fade even more.

My frown touched my kneecaps.

"What can I do to feed you right now?" I asked.

My soul pointed toward the door.

"Let's go outside. The way the light moves through the trees in the late Autumn is one of my favorite meals."

I nodded my head and opened the door and we went on to gorge ourselves under the resurrecting light like it was a chocolate fountain.

It was a harvest of blessings.

"Thank you," my glowing soul burped up to me through my veins. "This is exactly what I needed."

"Of course," I replied. "I'll do better, I promise. I'll give you a huge picnic every day."

My soul hugged my bones tightly and said "Well, then I guess I better go shopping."

"Shopping? For what?" I asked.

"For some stretchy pants."

Wonder*Flow*

I don't want to to sound out of touch,
but I really am repelled by the word *"influencer"*

that word suggests trying to
have control over somebody else

and there is already
too much of that going
in the world already

I don't like the term
"clout" either

that word is too fickle for me

whenever I desire power it feels like I'm
trying to hold a melting ice cube in my hand

I don't want to
sway anyone

I want to serve them

I don't want to
blaze a path for you

~ I want to get lost with you ~

to crave authority
would require me
□to surrender
my amateur status

and I quite love being
a newbie here with you here

I don't want to guide you down this River

I want to enjoy the ride with you
until we reach the great waterfall

don't follow me
flow with me

and as we go

let's not influence
each other to be like us

instead

let's listen to
each other

**until our ears become
shaped like our hearts**

Wonder *Wander* Two

I had to leave the path
to find my way

I had to get lost
to find God

I had to fall off the edge of the map
to find a home that changes its address
every time I take another step forward

however, before I did any of that

I spent most of my life searching
for peace by walking the same
worn path that everyone else
was taking

I was walking with everybody
as we followed the dusty trail
that we were told would lead
us to the promised river of life

we were like ants
marching together in line
through the desert

"Are we almost there?" I'd ask over and over

"Have faith," I was told by the lead ant

I got so thirsty

~so tired
~so scared

over time, I realized
that we were all just walking
in a great circle

"I think we've been here before," I'd comment

"Have faith," the lead ant would reply

"having faith"
in the ancient map
we were following
seemed like a luxury
for those who had
stronger spines

so, one night I slipped
out of line and off the path
and into the wide open vastness

and straight into the
uncharted territory of
my heart

- I've been in the wild
for so long
with only my heart as a
compass

that thumps harder whenever
I get close to an angel

and last night
my heart almost
burst through my

chest

yet,

I don't think that means
I'm getting closer to
what I'm searching for

because God isn't a destination
God is the journey

God isn't an "x!" in the ground
God is a "y?" on my tongue

The Divine is the sunlight peeking through
the deep woods I'm exploring

The Great Mystery is the soil
toes that squeezes through my toes
every time I sit down to watch the sunset

God is the endless horizon
that I am constantly chasing

God isn't a where
God is a here

I'm a nomad
whose principal
theology is to
never quit searching

I'm a member of the
church of seeking
hands

I believe in the canon of constant exploration

I'm lost in the vast expanse
of an undiscovered land of
exotic doubts and psalm-singing
owls who croon me to sleep
each night

I have no directions
except to where
my raging heart tells
me to go

I've left the map I was given in my youth

and now I'm considered "out there"
with the other heretics

however, I've learned
that the more I wander

the more wonderment I get to see

Wonder*Circle*

for those who came to Earth
to win and compete

will be terribly disappointed
when they find out

that life isn't
the Olympics

it's a gathering place

my love,

when we die we don't get
handed a bunch of trophies
by angels wearing stopwatches

there is no medal ceremony in the hereafter

there is just a campfire circle
where we make s'mores and
share our stories from Earth

the only game we play in
the afterlife is the one
where we take turns
listening to each other

~ and everyone always wins

Wonder*Ready*

"Come outside with me. It's so beautiful out here
and I have so much to show you," Miracle said.

Her hands wrapped around my wrist.
Tugging gently me to join her outside of my front door.

I couldn't.

The invisible line between being outside under the endless sky and inside with my
sadness felt like barbed wire. The threshold we were standing in was like thick
amber.

I was stuck.

I hated when Miracle showed up like this unannounced at my door. It was really
rude. It was presumptuous. It was without any social etiquette. Miracle never
could quite read the mood of the room.

It was just like her to show up after I had surrendered to my despair.

"I'd love to go outside with you but I can't,"
I told Miracle as I moved to break her hold on my wrist.

Her grip was tight.

Miracle kissed the top of my clenched fists
she was holding on to and asked:

"How come?" she asked softly.

I looked at Miracle and sighed. She was now covered in blue and red butterflies.
Her body was a tapestry of little wings opening and closing so deliberately.

How come??!!

What in the hell kind of question was that? How could she ask me that? Miracle knew the exact reason why I couldn't go outside with her.

It was the same reason I couldn't walk out the door with her yesterday or the countless days before that when she showed out up to invite me to go with her.

She was going to make me say it out loud. Fine. I would tell her exactly why I couldn't go outside with her. Anything for her to get bored and finally leave me alone for good.

"Because my depression won't let me!"
I shouted over the sound of her drumming butterfly wings.

"Why?" she asked.

I was full on angry now. I ripped my wrist out of her hand and moved to shut the door. Miracle's foot blocked it. I looked into her eyes that had become twin sunsets. They blazed like an endless autumn.

"Why what?" I asked sharply.

"Why do you keep asking your depression
for permission to live your life?"

I couldn't find an
answer to give her.

Which turned out
was my answer.

After a moment Miracle blanketed my hand with hers again. It was so warm. I could feel her veins writing a new gospel inside of me as our wrists twisted together like pretzel knots.

We spent ten minutes crying together before she gently pulled on my hand once more - indicating it was time for us to leave.

"Ready to go explore this world?" she asked.

I was.

I always had been.

Wonder*Chase*

I was riding comfortably
on the road to God

when suddenly
   and without warning

the wheels fell off of the
ornate carriage I was riding in

~ and I became stuck

I was stranded on a dusty road
surrounded by the untamed
wilderness on either side of me

"I have to get moving again," I thought

so, I spent way too much time
desperately trying to fix what was
irrecoverably broken

eventually, it became clear
that I would never get
my life to look the way it
used to

I was tempted to turn
the wreckage of my life
into a roadside museum

and to make a home
out of the ruins

but then suddenly
　and without warning

a blue butterfly came out
of the badlands next to me
~ and landed right on my nose

her wings had the most
abstract watercolor pattern
I had ever seen before

　~ but after spending an hour
watching her stretch and close her wings

I was able to see that the pattern
actually spelled three words that
I spoke out loud

"come find Me"

then suddenly
　and without warning

the butterfly leapt off of my nose and
back into the sprawling wild

I immediately set fire to the
wreckage of my broken down carriage and
　I chased the butterfly straight into
the chaos of the wilderness

I've been out here
for years now

and I've learned
that no matter how lost I

have gotten

I have never felt more
found by the Great Love

I have learned
that there is no
set road for me to
journey to the home of God

for me, God's home isn't a fabulous destination
at the end of a detailed map or tight travel schedule

God's home is the uncharted
dangerous expanse of wonder
and howling wolves

where the two of us
climb trees to scout
the next day's walk

I was never going
to find Love by
watching the wheels
spin on a groomed path

I was only going
to find God by
stepping off the path
and into the crackerjack
splendor of the mystery
that has been calling
to me for years

it's an undiscovered
land where tree trunks
are shaped like question marks

and rivers lead me from one
curiosity to the next

it's a relentless and unending
adventure

where Spirit arranges a couple hundred
 bright blue butterflies in the sky to
spell the same thing each morning:

"Come find me"

Wonder*Eyes*

~ I've wandered
into wonderment

to make a home
out of the *unknown*

~ I've let go of
my need for directions

and now feel peace
deep in my *bones*

~ I can now hear
God calling me

from a pay phone
inside my old *heart*

~ I can smell the morning dew
in my eyes

as my life has been
given a brand new *start*

~ I'm looking at everything
with the eyes of a child

these days even a single blade
of grass holds my *gaze*

~ I've fed my calendar
to the wind

now a single minute can
last for several *days*

~ I was told once that the
devil's in the details

but, my love, I've recently
learned that is most *untrue*

~ because I've found the divine
in every pore of your skin

and the way each ray of sun
effortlessly reflects off of *you*

~ I don't know where
I'm going

I'm a satellite lost
in time and *space*

~ I left the orbit of
earthly certainty

to chase a UFO
of sacred *grace*

~ I'm not afraid of what
I haven't discovered yet

and if I turn up missing
please know where I'll *be*

I'll have headed inward
to explore myself

in the anointed wilds
that exist inside of *me*

~ I've wandered
into wonderment

and let my best laid
plans become *history*

~ I'm waltzing straight
into a strange holy fog

to embrace the
adventure of the *mystery*

~ see you later
see you someday *soon*
~ my new forwarding zip code

is the somewhere on the *moon*

Wonder*Concert*

every night before I go to sleep
I invite all of my beloveds who have
died to join me around my bed to
sing with me

when I was younger
 the attendance was sparse

it was like a barbershop quartet
of a few deceased loved ones and me

squeaking out a few
sweet improvised tunes
about the miracles of
this life and afterlife

In the echo chamber of
my quieting heart

                              but now that I'm older

The more crowded my
bedroom is getting

and the louder the
singing has gotten

lately some of my beloveds
are even bringing their instruments
to play around my bed

it's not a seance

it's a symphony

there are so
many beloveds
showing up to
help me compose

that I've had to ask
them to stand close
to each other

now, at bedtime

my packed bedroom has become
a bustling concert hall

some nights we play
the rock and roll of
gratitude

and some nights we all
hold classical violins and
play songs about
the energy of love
that radiates out
of the beating heart
of the universe

some nights we play the jazz
of how wonderfully terrifying it
can be to give our hearts
to each other

some nights we
sing acapella

some nights

we just hum

it doesn't really matter
what style we choose
to play

because with every chord
this community of
beloved ghosts and
I create together

the less afraid of death I become

as it turns out
this adventure we
are on together

is all music

**and the beat goes
on and on and on and...**

Wonder *Wisp*

inside each of us

is a little wisp of energy

that sparked to life on

the very first day we

were imagined into existence

then somehow we slipped under the skin

of these weird little bodies we navigate

as these bursts of light

we became captains

of these fleshy vessels

asked to explore our

earthly universe without

ever being given a map

we fly around like fireflies

against the dark canvas of the sooty unknown

~ as we buzz around

sometimes we dance together in harmony as if synchronized by the same engineer

sometimes we bump into each other in conflict pursuing some imaginary contest

victory

sometimes we get lost in the pitch dark and our light feels like it will never be seen

to be these little freckles of energy operating a body is such a tricky thing to do

and it's easy to forget that we are more than our skin and bone vessels

we are a swarm of miracles
searching for meaning
in the wildlands of this world we were sent to

and I believe maybe the purpose for us here is finding a way to connect the inner
light inside of us to one another

I'm considering that we are meant to be pulsing Christmas lights on the same
string instead of standalone static bulbs?

my love, I have come to believe that we are all born of the same cosmic signal fire
that was lit billions of years ago

maybe our mission is to bridge the space between each other
to grow together and ignite that fire here on Earth?

I think we got it wrong
hell isn't about flames

heaven is

and I can't wait to someday
slip out of my body
and build that eternal campfire with you

A Final Postcard From the Edge of Wonder

My heart had been my shelter

for so many years—

a place I could hide from the world.

But one day, the wind blew so hard

that the roof of my heart came right off,

and the walls fell down.

I became unprotected, so vulnerable to the world.

And I got hurt over and over,

until I figured out that most of my pain

was due to me trying to rebuild my heart

on the exact same spot it collapsed on.

Well, if I am being honest, I didn't really "figure anything out."

My heart just told me

that I had to let go of how it

used to look if the two of us

were going to stay together.

"I don't want to be a shelter anymore,"

my heart announced while we were walking

together in an open field.

"What do you want to be?" I asked.

"A hot air balloon," it replied,

as it started to slowly rise up.

"Why?"

My heart started to slowly rise up above the flowers

and softly said:

"So I can chase wonder."

So, I built a basket and jumped inside of it.

Now the two of us are traveling together—

two seekers who don't really know

what it is we are looking for.

Where are we going?

Towards wonder.

Always towards wonder.

Grateful For The Company

My beloved fellow seeker, thank you for joining me in the wilds of my wandering wonderment. I'm so very grateful you held my hand as we walked into the fog. Knowing that I am not alone on this journey has made me feel so much braver.

After all of our searching under rocks and behind twisted trees, I don't know if I am any closer to answering life's greatest riddles.

Maybe though - we aren't supposed to solve every mystery? Perhaps the answers we try and discern are not nearly as important as the questions we ask.

Maybe we are meant to be lost in the woods? Maybe that is where God is looking for us anyway? Maybe our hearts are compasses where wonder is set as our true north? Maybe that's why our hearts ache so much? Maybe that is the howl of hope that keeps calling us to keep following the arrow that points to a flowing mystery instead of a concrete certainty?

Maybe we are meant to be endless seekers of miracles? Maybe our journey hasn't come to an end after all? If that's the case - let's keep holding hands. I think I hear a song playing in the wind right now. Come chase it with me! Let's see where we end up!

Let's keep following the wonder to WHEREVER it leads!

About the Poet

John Roedel is a fourth generation Wyomingite improv comic. He began writing poetry in 2017 when the words he was stuffing in his pillowcase heart had nowhere else to go. Much to his surprise, John's heartfelt words began to circulate around the world in 2020. Offering a sincere and very relatable look at his faith crisis, mental health, personal struggles, perception of our world, and even his fashion sense, John's writing has been shared millions of times across social media and lauded by fans and readers worldwide.

Previously this penguin-shaped poet has published six books: *Hey God. Hey John.*, *Any Given Someday*, *Untied*, *Remedy*, *Upon Departure* and *Fitting In Is For Sardines*.

John teaches at universities and retreat centers across the US, blending his trademark comedy with creative exercises, journaling, dialogue, and introspection to help people fearlessly embrace and share their personal stories.

For more information on John's work, retreat offerings or booking availability please visit johnroedel.com

Made in United States
Troutdale, OR
11/14/2024

24819193R10120